FIND YOUR SUCCESS CODE

ARVIND UPADHYAY

Success provides confidence, security, a sense of well-being, the ability to contribute at a greater level, hope and leadership. Without success, you, the group, your company, your goals, dreams and even entire civilizations cease to survive. We want to achieve success because it is a part of our life plans. Success is strongly related with our life plans. We can distinguish certain milestones in our plans, like graduating, getting a desired job, starting our own business or new relationship.

As I conducted my research on success, I realized that in society there are two different definitions. There is a first group of people who think that success means "be happy with what you have, no matter what fate has in store for us; do the best you can with the hand you're dealt". For these people, success appears to be a feeling of contentment with what they have managed to achieve in life. They tell the great difficulties they've overcome and end by telling you that, all things considered, what they have is all they could have possibly achieved, and are therefore satisfied with what they have built. In some cases they will make comparisons between themselves and those who are worse, saying "I shouldn't expect more. I'm happy with what I have. True, I don't have much, but there are those who have even less." Although they are maybe contented these are not the people I want to talk about. We're not talking about them because their lives, although balanced, are based on the concept of "barely enough." When you ask them how they're doing, they generally respond with "pretty good." They are people who earn "enough" (but not as much as they truly need in order to realize their dreams), have companies that are doing "OK", that is, "if there are no major upheavals, if all the customers pay at the end of the month, if none of the salespeople quit" then the company is fine. If something goes wrong, then they have problems. I do not know why, but that "barely enough" mentality always seems precarious to me. A kind of "all is well as long as there are no problems." A delicate balance, beyond which things could easily go wrong. In this book we will talk instead about the second definition of success: "The knowledge that you are materializing your dreams". Because success really is just that. It is not based on the concept of barely enough, but on the concept of ABUNDANCE. Abundance means having much more than what you could ever need. Abundance in a relationship does not mean having three wives, or a wife and two lovers (though this book will do wonders for you, it won't be taking things quite that far). But it does mean having such a good relationship with your partner that a disagreement, a fight, or your absence for fifteen days for work, will not in any way reduce the esteem, affection and harmony that exists between the two of you. By professional abundance, it means earning a lot more than your financial needs technically require. It means having so many customers interested in your product or service that you have trouble getting to them all, it means that even an overdue bill or nonpayment by an important customer will not have any affect on the survival of your company. In short, abundance does not mean a delicate balance on which your survival depends; it means that things are really going well... not just "sort of ok".However much the above may seem obvious, today a majority of businesses live with the concept of "sort of ok". 63% of the population thinks that they could materialize their dreams only if they win the lottery. Many business owners tell me that "things will be better when the economy recovers", the majority of managers have considerable problems with staff, in short, things are "sort of ok" nearly everywhere. I do not want to generalize the situation, but frankly, all this "sort of ok", all this "things aren't that bad, there are those who are worse off", to me, it means only one thing: the culture of success is being lost. People who were once idealistic, who chased their dreams, have become "realistic" people, with their feet firmly on the ground, spouting phrases such as "it's not that simple", and "easier said than done". Looking more closely at all these people who have embraced the "sort of ok" culture, we can also deduce something else: they too, at one time, chased their dreams. They too saw success as abundance. Then, probably, something happened that caused them to change their definition of success, which made them move from the group of definition #2 (the realization of their dreams) to definition #1 (be satisfied with what you have). Well, this book is against the "sort of ok" culture. This book maintains that, if you truly want to, you can accomplish your dreams. That there is no need to act like Aesop's fox with the grapes1, and insist that success or abundance aren't things that really interest you. All of us, when we're at our best, seek abundance. ? What parent, faced with their child's illness, would not insist, no matter the cost, on consulting the best specialists in the world? ? What salesperson would not want, at least for a moment, to have the highest sales in the company? ? What business owner would not love, even if only for a day, for their company to be the undisputed leader of the market? ? What minimum-wage employee has never fantasized about owning the home of their dreams? Nice little fairy tales, you might say. No. It is the "sort of ok" culture that is taking root in society so firmly, that it is taking away the one thing that has always been crucial: our dreams. In this book I will not give you a recipe to make "sort of ok" more palatable, instead I will talk about abundance. How to build the life you've always dreamed of. The book is organized into three parts. In the first, we'll talk about how to stop being invisible, the condition that results from your personal shortcomings and prevents you from being visible to the people who can provide opportunities you need to change your life. In the second part I will talk about how to toughen yourself up, in order to overcome any difficulties you may encounter in the path to success, and in the third and final part I will cover the subject of real success.The text is full of information and ideas that you can apply immediately to change yourself and your life. I suggest you read it for the first time from start to finish, taking notes or highlighting things you need to change or start doing. Then re-read the rules in which you feel you need to improve several times, as much as it takes for you to start putting them into practice. I assure you that, following the ten rules, your life will take a definite turn for the better. Believe me, achieving abundance is not just a matter of wealth or real estate. It is, first of all, a matter of satisfaction and happiness: a person dies when their last dream dies. If you have fallen into the "sort of ok" culture, then you are dying piece by piece. You may have every justification in the world, and you might even try to convince me, but the problem remains that, deep down, not even you believe your own excuses. Like all human beings, you seek and deserve abundance. This book will teach you to reach it, and to become a champion in whatever business you have chosen. With my best wishes,

ARVIND UPADHYAY

Contents

Foreword *ix*

1. Stop Following False Leads! 1

2. To Be Successful You Have To Improve The Quality Of Your Exchange 6

3. Understand, Meet, And Exceed The Expectations Of Others! 14

4. Become A Great Human Being! 22

5. The Turning Point 33

6. If You Want Things To Change, First You Have To Change Yourself 37

7. Become A Leader! 43

8. The Companions You Choose Determine Your Destiny: Avoid Toxic People 49

9. The Materialization Of Success Create Your Future! 54

10. The Success Of An Individual Is Measured By The Success Of Those Around Them 69

Foreword

Success is not an escape from a life that does not satisfy you. Success is a transformation of an unsatisfying existence into something great. However, this transformation is internal rather than external: the transformation of your personality.It will not happen overnight (we must remember the concept of time perspective), but, as Aristotle said, just a little at a time, doing different things, you can savor the gratification that comes from witnessing one of nature's most extraordinary miracles: your transformation into an attractive and successful personality. With an attractive personality, you'll start to notice that all the opportunities I've mentioned, were all around you even yesterday, but you simply didn't see them until recently.As a child, my parents would take me to the beach. Sometimes, if I had a rubber all, I would entertain myself by trying to shove the ball as far underwater as I could. Inevitably, the push of the water would always bring it back up to the surface, often even causing it to fly into the air. If I wanted to keep it underwater I had to exert extraordinary power, because the natural condition of the ball was not meant to stay under. This example fits perfectly with the concept of success. Success is like the ball that flies out of the water. Humans, in their natural condition as attractive and positive people, can ONLY be successful. To have no success requires the constant application of a counterforce: the fact of being in violation of simple, almost invisible, natural laws that govern life.l you see your prosperity increase, not only will you see the people around you begin to smile, to be happy and to win, but you will also have regained something that previously no one had considered of importance: yourself. You are important because the world, in order to become a better place, needs YOUR support too. Your dreams are important. Your aspirations are important. You are important. Always remember that.

CHAPTER ONE

Stop Following False Leads!

A person who feels themselves falling into the "sort of ok" culture, in an attempt to put things right, will sometimes start looking for red herrings. They do this by looking for that one opportunity, the amazing discovery that will allow them to become suddenly extremely rich or successful, and change their life 180 degrees. This is why you see employees checking recruitment ads every week, hoping to find the right opportunity, that one company that will give them the chance they need. You see salespeople constantly searching for the winning product, that one really cool and innovative product, that once launched will be in great demand and bring them huge commissions. You see business owners looking to earn money on the stock market rather than with their company. You also see a great flourish of magazines raving about all the latest and greatest entrepreneurial opportunities: ostrich herding, take up flipping houses, open a bar in Costa Rica, launch a successful app, and so on. I do not mean to criticize all of these initiatives, and I absolutely do not want to criticize those who think you should try to find the right opportunity that will allow you to be successful. At least these people haven't yet fallen into the gray world of realists. They're stilling trying to resist the "sort of ok". They still have some kind of dream. But you know what? These people will never reach success. They'll never reach it because they'll never find that perfect opportunity, as long as they continue to look for it in the wrong place. Like me twelve years ago, seeking opportunities in newspapers, in magazines, in the job market, at employment agencies. They're looking in the wrong place. Whatever opportunities there may be, in the end they prove themselves to be red herrings. It will just be yet another disappointment that pushes them further into the world of "kind of ok". The real opportunity, actually needs to be something you find inside yourself. When you don't succeed, the quality of the opportunity isn't the problem, YOU are the problem. It may be that someone can manage to build a thriving business breeding ostriches or flipping houses, but the emphasis is on the wrong thing. The emphasis is put on the activities that they have chosen, when, in fact, it matters very little. What really matters is the fact that they had developed what I call "the successful personality." It is this, rather than the activity itself, which allows people to reach their goals. Until you develop a successful personality, all the opportunities that you try to chase will just end up being red herrings. This is why I say that by looking externally, outside yourself, you are looking in the wrong place. If you want to succeed, if you want to achieve a state of abundance, you first need to work on developing a successful personality. It will be this personality, more than anything else, that allows you to stop being invisible, this state of inconsequence that prevents people from involving you in the really interesting projects that could bring you abundance. It is this personality that will sharpen 9 your vision and more clearly show you which opportunities are the right ones to take advantage of. Like all of us, you possess skills that you only partially use. Once you have developed these skills and your successful personality, you'll find that you no longer have to search for opportunities, they will simply appear before you whenever you need them. Think for a moment: every day on this planet, transactions for billions of dollars are conducted. Every day millions of business people seek partners or collaborators to offer opportunities in exchange for help. Every day customers seek suppliers to entrust with contracts worth billions. Have you ever wondered why none of these activities involve you? The answer, my friend, is that you're invisible. There is something in your way of being and doing that causes these people to not even think of involving you. If you start to look for opportunities like crazy, without making fundamental changes to your personality, you will continue to experience failure after failure. Until one day you find yourself looking at someone warily when they try to talk to you about success. I hate to tell you this, but at this point you'll be just another face in the crowd of lottery ticket consumers. Some may object that it is necessary to search for new opportunities, because obviously whatever they're doing now isn't working. To these people I can say, unequivocally, that WHAT they do isn't the problem, THEY are the problem! I still remember my very first day at work. The personnel manager asked me what areas of the company I liked most. I replied that I liked everything except HR and sales. Well... I've spent my entire life working just in those areas! Among the successful people we see every day, many have arrived at their line of work not because they sought it out, but by sheer chance. A dear friend and client of mine directs one of the leading companies in home security systems. One day I asked him why he had decided to go into that area. He told me that several years earlier, the company of one of his clients had gone bankrupt and they couldn't pay him, instead they paid him off with a few thousand dollars worth of security equipment. In order not to lose money, my friend decided to sell it and so began a career that led him to great success. Henry Ford himself wanted to break into the world of watches before he started producing cars! Some might even say that "you are actually meant to do something else, the profession of your dreams must be in some other area." Watch out for these thoughts, if you have them, because they are your enemies. Years ago, I liked public relations and dreamed of a career as a consultant in that field, but at the end I became tremendously successful at something else. I know an entrepreneur of great success in the financial industry, whose original ambition was to manage a farm! I'm not asking to stifle your dreams. As we shall see, these are very important, but at the same time you must realize that success is not an escape from an unsatisfying life, instead, it is the gradual transformation of an existence that doesn't currently satisfy you into something bigger and better. Materializing your dreams, in other words, means first passing through the phase where you appreciate and excel in what you do NOW. Only in this way will you become a successful person. Then, trust me, a person who is successful and knows the rules, can repeat it in other areas (in the end, even the financial industry 9 your vision and more clearly show you which opportunities are the right ones to take advantage of. Like all of us, you possess skills that you only partially use. Once you have developed these skills and your successful personality, you'll find that you no longer have to search for opportunities, they will simply appear before you whenever you need them. Think for a moment: every day on this planet, transactions for billions of dollars are conducted. Every day millions of business people seek partners or collaborators to offer opportunities in exchange for help. Every day customers seek suppliers to entrust with contracts worth billions. Have you ever wondered why none of these activities involve you? The answer, my friend, is that you're invisible. There is something in your way of being and doing that causes these people to not even think of involving you. If you start to look for opportunities like crazy, without making fundamental changes to your personality, you will continue to experience failure after failure. Until one day you find yourself looking at someone warily when they try to talk to you about success. I hate to tell you this, but at this point you'll be just another face in the crowd of lottery ticket consumers. Some may object that it is necessary to search for new opportunities, because obviously whatever they're doing now isn't working. To these people I can say, unequivocally, that WHAT they do isn't the problem, THEY are the problem! I still remember my very first day at work. The personnel manager asked me what areas of the company I liked most. I replied that I liked everything except HR and sales. Well... I've spent my entire life working just in those areas! Among the successful people we see every day, many have arrived at their line of work not because they sought it out, but by sheer chance. A dear friend and client of mine directs one of the leading companies in home security systems. One day I asked him why he had decided to go into that area. He told me that several years earlier, the company of one of his clients had gone bankrupt and they couldn't pay him, instead they paid him off with a few thousand dollars worth of security equipment. In order not to lose money, my friend decided to sell it and so began a career that led him to great success. Henry Ford himself wanted to break into the world of watches before he started producing cars! Some might even say that "you are actually meant to do something else, the profession of your dreams must be in some other area." Watch out for these thoughts, if you have them, because they are your enemies. Years ago, I liked public relations and dreamed of a career as a consultant in that field, but at the end I became tremendously successful at something else. I know an entrepreneur of great success in the financial industry, whose original ambition was to manage a farm! I'm not asking to stifle your dreams. As we shall see, these are very important, but at the same time you must realize that success is not an escape from an unsatisfying life, instead, it is the gradual transformation of an existence that doesn't currently satisfy you into something bigger and better. Materializing your dreams, in other words, means first passing through the phase where you appreciate and excel in what you do NOW. Only in this way will you become a successful person. Then, trust me, a person who is successful and knows the rules, can repeat it in other areas (in the end, even the financial industry 10 entrepreneur managed to get his farm, but first he had to flourish with his financial company). You must not stop dreaming. You simply have to stop looking outside of yourself for something that you already have inside you: the ingredients of a successful personality. As you get to know these ingredients, stop chasing false leads and instead commit to excelling in your current profession. You'll see that these ingredients will not only lead you to the right opportunities, not only remove your invisibility and bring you abundance, but also give you a much better life. With the second, third and fourth rule I will help you to build a successful personality so you stop being invisible and get involved in real opportunities. UNTIL YOU BUILD A SUCCESSFUL PERSONALITY, ALL THE LEADS YOU ATTEMPT TO FOLLOW WILL PROVE FALSE.

CHAPTER TWO

To be successful you have to improve the quality of your exchange

"Your success in life depends largely on your ability to become an expert in a particular area and provide outstanding service in that area". Napoleon Hill We live in a world that is based on exchange. Human and business relationships are based on the pillars of exchange. This is not to say that charity or a desire to help others without ulterior motives is not important, quite the contrary. However, as human beings, we are at the center of countless exchanges with other people. Analyzing the "trades" in which a person is involved, we can understand a lot about why their life is going well or badly. Unsuccessful are generally trying to "manipulate" exchanges in which they are involved in order to get more by giving less. Truly successful people instead realize that if they want to have a greater return from others, they must improve the value or quantity of what they provide. At the lowest end of the scale we find the con man. He believes that to get more out of life he just needs to "package it well" for other people so that they agree to give something of great value (in most cases money) in exchange for something that is worth little or nothing. However his attempt may go, we all know that his life style is full of ups and downs and poor economic conditions, not to mention the risk of prison. The con man, however, is not the only person trying to artificially manipulate their exchanges in order to get more out of the system while giving next to nothing. There are also several companies that base their success solely on their sales pitch and customer acquisition, rather than on any real service or product of value (as can be seen, for example, in many "pyramid schemes"). Then there are people who try to speculate: speculate on the stock market, oil, gold, or flipping houses. They often talk about their great trades but they rarely talk about the heavy losses they have also suffered. Then there are people who think they can "work around" the harsh laws of exchange by inventing that new app that will change the world... "I'll start breeding ostriches because their meat is expensive and this way I'll earn a lot of money." Dreaming or inventing is great but without putting in the hard work is never going to be good enough. Even more common are those who continue to demand things from others without giving anything in return. I've got nothing against inventors. What I'm criticizing are the people who try to circumvent the laws of give and take, to strive to get more with less, people who hope to reach abundance by artificially manipulating the exchange. These people, contrary to the common belief that they are smart or clever, not only never achieve prosperity, but often also live a miserable and boring life. I'm not the first to advocate the importance of exchanges in human relations. Many before me have studied the subject, from Ralph Waldo Emerson to Jim Rohn. Emerson, in his 11 RULE 2 To be successful you have to improve the quality of your exchange "Your success in life depends largely on your ability to become an expert in a particular area and provide outstanding service in that area". Napoleon Hill We live in a world that is based on exchange. Human and business relationships are based on the pillars of exchange. This is not to say that charity or a desire to help others without ulterior motives is not important, quite the contrary. However, as human beings, we are at the center of countless exchanges with other people. Analyzing the "trades" in which a person is involved, we can understand a lot about why their life is going well or badly. Unsuccessful are generally trying to "manipulate" exchanges in which they are involved in order to get more by giving less. Truly successful people instead realize that if they want to have a greater return from others, they must improve the value or quantity of what they provide. At the lowest end of the scale we find the con man. He believes that to get more out of life he just needs to "package it well" for other people so that they agree to give something of great value (in most cases money) in exchange for something that is worth little or nothing. However his attempt may go, we all know that his life style is full of ups and downs and poor economic conditions, not to mention the risk of prison. The con man, however, is not the only person trying to artificially manipulate their exchanges in order to get more out of the system while giving next to nothing. There are also several companies that base their success solely on their sales pitch and customer acquisition, rather than on any real service or product of value (as can be seen, for example, in many "pyramid schemes"). Then there are people who try to speculate: speculate on the stock market, oil, gold, or flipping houses. They often talk about their great trades but they rarely talk about the heavy losses they have also suffered. Then there are people who think they can "work around" the harsh laws of exchange by inventing that new app that will change the world... "I'll start breeding ostriches because their meat is expensive and this way I'll earn a lot of money." Dreaming or inventing is great but without putting in the hard work is never going to be good enough. Even more common are those who continue to demand things from others without giving anything in return. I've got nothing against inventors. What I'm criticizing are the people who try to circumvent the laws of give and take, to strive to get more with less, people who hope to reach abundance by artificially manipulating the exchange. These people, contrary to the common belief that they are smart or clever, not only never achieve prosperity, but often also live a miserable and boring life. I'm not the first to advocate the importance of exchanges in human relations. Many before me have studied the subject, from Ralph Waldo Emerson to Jim Rohn. Emerson, in his 12 famous Essay on Compensation, at the end of the 1800s already claimed: "You will be paid for exactly what you have done, not more, not less. In work and in life you can not cheat. The thief steals from himself, the con man cheats himself." Emerson called this theory "the absolute balance of give and take, the doctrine that everything has its price and if that price is not paid, you get something else and not the thing that you thought" and used it to indicate that a person who tries to circumvent the laws of exchange, no matter how "clever" they may be, won't get anywhere. Whenever you receive while giving little or nothing in return, you experience a trauma on a motivational level One of the most strongly felt problems of business owners is the generational shift. In most cases, when the children succeed their parents in the management of the company, it begins to decline and then closes. This itself is strange, considering that the children of these business owners should have had access to better education, have led a more comfortable life, not so full of hardship or difficulty as their parents, have grown up in a better environment. The problem is that often they received so much without producing anything, and are so used to an exchange in which things are simply "owed" to them. This causes them to lose sight of something's true value. What kind of leader could a person ever be if they think that everything is simply their due? Take another example of people who receive without giving anything in return: fortune tellers and psychics. They can earn a lot of money while giving nothing in return, except at best a bit of hope. Have you ever studied the expression on the face of these people? As already said by Ralph Waldo Emerson in his famous Essay on compensation, the person who receives without giving anything in return, gets only sadness, negativity and a life of misery. In any case, we don't want to talk about other people, we're supposed to be talking about you. Deep down, like everyone, you want to help others, to contribute to their improvement and happiness, you want to have an important part in the success of the company you're in. True, receiving money for nothing can be a pleasant experience, but after that how do you feel? Deep down you're left with a bitter taste in your mouth. It would have been a hundred times better if you had earned it. Successful people don't try to avoid the basic principles of living, don't seek to earn or gain money by manipulating exchange, but instead provide something of great value. If that isn't immediately possible, instead of looking for the "next amazing opportunity" that will prove to be yet another false trail, they work on themselves to improve so that they are then able to produce value. Exchange A farmer is out in the field. The morning starts at 5:00AM, and the plowing, hoeing, seeding, watering, and killing parasites goes on and on until, one day a few months later, a basket full of tomatoes is ready to go to the market. The tomatoes are exchanged for cash or other assets that allow for survival. All of us would consider it bizarre if a farmer tried to go to market without tomatoes, and still demanded 13 money just because they had dug, planted, watered, and so on. "Well, good for you," we might tell him, "but we're only giving you money if you have tomatoes." As absurd as the example may seem, it makes a point that is still very present for most people in society. People who attempt to go to market with nothing but their actions, rather than the results of their actions. They claim they should receive money in exchange for action, time, commitment, effort, WITHOUT PRODUCING ANY RESULT. There are employees who think their salary is owed to them simply because of the hours they spend at work, for the effort they put into the things they do, for the school degree they have achieved with great diligence, for the position they hold within the company hierarchy... but where are the tomatoes? The employee who earns a lot is not necessarily the one that works hardest or takes the most on. Instead they are people who, more than others, produce results through their efforts. An employee in the accounting department is not paid for the hours they spend in the office, but for the money they collect from customers; a teacher is not paid for the hours spent teaching or explaining, but for actually instilling new skills in their students; a warehouse manager is not paid for the hours spent stocking and moving boxes, but for the rapidity with which they provide goods to those who need them, for the cleanliness and order of the warehouse, for their accuracy in avoiding of shortages. The examples are endless. There are salespeople who think they are doing well because they sell a lot to their clients. This is partially true, but a truly successful salesperson is one that helps THE CLIENT TO BE BETTER OFF. The successful salesperson isn't the one that fills the customer's warehouse with a bunch of stuff, rather it is the one that ensures the client in turn resells what they bought in large volume and earns a lot of money. Consequently teaching the client how to properly use the products they purchased, teaching them how to run the business, how to advertise, how to sell a lot. Sometimes I see consultants or technicians involved in client companies, but their interventions do not give any result. Sometimes they try to get away with being paid without providing anything in return, just for the fact that they spent so much time at the company. But again, where are the tomatoes? Many people today claim to exchange their time or effort in exchange for money or something else. They will not go anywhere. You must exchange RESULTS. ACTIONS WITHOUT RESULTS ARE WORTH ABSOLUTELY NOTHING. So, if you want, you can even try that new business breeding ostriches. Perhaps it's a good idea and maybe ostrich meat isn't so bad, but know that your business will succeed not because you hang a sign that says you now sell ostrich meat, or because you put a beautiful Instagram video. Instead, it is specifically because you were able to make the ostrich meat a GOOD DEAL for your customer. What is the result you produce and exchange when you do business with people? What is the great deal people are getting when they choose to work with you? 13 money just because they had dug, planted, watered, and so on. "Well, good for you," we might tell him, "but we're only giving you money if you have tomatoes." As absurd as the example may seem, it makes a point that is still very present for most people in society. People who attempt to go to market with nothing but their actions, rather than the results of their actions. They claim they should receive money in exchange for action, time, commitment, effort, WITHOUT PRODUCING ANY RESULT. There are employees who think their salary is owed to them simply because of the hours they spend at work, for the effort they put into the things they do, for the school degree they have achieved with great diligence, for the position they hold within the company hierarchy... but where are the tomatoes? The employee who earns a lot is not necessarily the one that works hardest or takes the most on. Instead they are people who, more than others, produce results through their efforts. An employee in the accounting department is not paid for the hours they spend in the office, but for the money they collect from customers; a teacher is not paid for the hours spent teaching or explaining, but for actually instilling new skills in their students; a warehouse manager is not paid for the hours spent stocking and moving boxes, but for the rapidity with which they provide goods to those who need them, for the cleanliness and order of the warehouse, for their accuracy in avoiding of shortages. The examples are endless. There are salespeople who think they are doing well because they sell a lot to their clients. This is partially true, but a truly successful salesperson is one that helps THE CLIENT TO BE BETTER OFF. The successful salesperson isn't the one that fills the customer's warehouse with a bunch of stuff, rather it is the one that ensures the client in turn resells what they bought in large volume and earns a lot of money. Consequently teaching the client how to properly use the products they purchased, teaching them how to run the business, how to advertise, how to sell a lot. Sometimes I see consultants or technicians involved in client companies, but their interventions do not give any result. Sometimes they try to get away with being paid without providing anything in return, just for the fact that they spent so much time at the company. But again, where are the tomatoes? Many people today claim to exchange their time or effort in exchange for money or something else. They will not go anywhere. You must exchange RESULTS. ACTIONS WITHOUT RESULTS ARE WORTH ABSOLUTELY NOTHING. So, if you want, you can even try that new business breeding ostriches. Perhaps it's a good idea and maybe ostrich meat isn't so bad, but know that your business will succeed not because you hang a sign that says you now sell ostrich meat, or because you put a beautiful Instagram video. Instead, it is specifically because you were able to make the ostrich meat a GOOD DEAL for your customer. What is the result you produce and exchange when you do business with people? What is the great deal people are getting when they choose to work with you? 14 Answering this question is not just a matter of finance, your earnings, but primarily a question of personal well-being. If you insist on providing something that has little value or try to make exchanges based on actions or effort and not results, bit by bit you yourself will be the one that burns out.

You'll get used to receiving by giving little or nothing in return, and you'll cripple your basic personality, which is at its heart a positive personality, oriented towards help and contribution. And what do you mutate into? An unfortunate and ineffective person. Stop trying to manipulate exchange artificially. Stop giving in to the allure of receiving things in exchange for results of little value. Accept your basic personality, the personality of success, get in touch with your deeper qualities and refuse money offered to you when you have not given something of value in exchange. Not only you will be successful, but you'll be immensely better off. You can do it Twenty-five years ago I did not earn much. In fact let's face it, I was dirt poor. There was a time in my life that constituted a turning point. My parents lent me money and although they told me that one day I would have to repay them, I had never been pressed to do so. Well, one day I showed up at their door and said, "Now let's do the math. Tell me exactly how much I owe you, how much you have lent me all these years". My mother, like any generous parent, told me that the money wasn't a problem, they were just fine without it. I insisted on making a list and then we established a monthly amount for the return. From then on I refused to receive more money from them, even though at times I had my own difficulties. I still remember that when I left I was happy, because I felt I had done the right thing, even though I was full of doubts. Would I make it? Could I stand on my own two legs? From there I began to earn more and more, and now it's been years since I worried about money, such is the abundance that I managed to create in my life. Today, I feel the same way about exchange. If I don't provide the results, then I don't want the money. This view is, in itself, a disruptive force. It forces you to get back to your basic skills, it forces you to innovate, to study, to get busy, and is perhaps one of the most powerful weapons to achieve success. Money Money is a symbol that represents what, in the past, we physically provided to the market (by "market", I mean the exchange we make with customers, employers, colleagues, etc.). The $100 in the farmer's pocket is just a symbol of the tomatoes they produced and sold. The money you have at the moment only represents the results or products that you provided to the market in the past. Money is not a cause, but an effect. A result of what you have been able to provide. If you want more money, you shouldn't look for systems to artificially manipulate the principles of exchange, but try to provide something that has more value to the market. But the greatest value, however strange it may seem, is not something you will find by searching out the "perfect" opportunity, or discovering a new and innovative product that 15 everyone will buy. High value is produced by maintaining your basic personality and working to make a deal for your customer or any business relationship you may develop. It is produced by studying, taking care of the person, assisting them, helping them, and working hard, but this will be the topic of the next rule. Success Success is the act of moving to a higher level of exchange. That's all. It is not chasing the chimera, the latest trends in terms of opportunity, it is not about making a good impression at the job interview for that fantastic company that has promised $150,000 per year, it is not about guessing which shares will rise in the stock market. Success is moving to a higher level of exchange, a level at which what you provide to other people has a much, much greater value than what you receive for it. This will not only take you straight in the world of abundance, but, more importantly, will allow you to rehabilitate and revive the great person, the star player, the slumbering giant, that you have inside: YOURSELF. It's time to get to work. Where are the tomatoes?

Understand, meet, and exceed the expectations of others!

"Reap what you sow. What we put into the universe is what comes back to us." The Buddhist Law of Cause and Effect. Once you have decided to dedicate yourself to your profession, stop chasing after false leads, and have decided to improve the quality of your exchange, you will already have the first ingredients you need to develop a successful personality. Not only that, the dedication obtained will also allow you to materialize the third rule of success: understand, meet, and exceed the expectations of others! Wealth depends on the value of what you provide to the market The wealth of Bill Gates does not depend on luck, but due to the fact that he has provided the market with something extremely valuable: the ability to use a computer to simplify personal and professional life. Without Microsoft Word, writing this book would have taken me at least twice as long. I am therefore willing to pay Microsoft a fraction of the time it saves me, that is to say, the price of the Word program. As mentioned in the second rule, the first secret of money is just that: to have money you need to provide something of value to your customer or to your boss in exchange. The larger the value perceived by that person, the more willing they will be to give you money. The money that you own today is nothing more than an indicator of how much value you have been able to provide to the market in the past. If you don't have very much, the problem is not the market that pays you less than you're worth, but in most cases it is the fact that you do not understand what the market considers of value. Understanding the expectations Most people living in the "sort of ok" culture don't understand the actual expectations of their exchange partners, indeed they don't care to even consider them. Instead they pay much closer attention to their OWN expectations. Almost every book that talks about job interviews refers the fact that perhaps the biggest mistake a candidate can make is to immediately ask about the salary. These books teach us that when we're trying to get hired, more than anything else we should try to understand what the needs of the employer are and show them how we are the person to meet those needs. Any book on "Sales" worth its salt says that a good salesperson, if they want to sell well, must forget their own expectations (closing the sale) during negotiations, and try to understand the needs and expectations of the potential customer. Many books tell us that just this simple action can be enough to increase sales.However, despite the many books on the subject, today almost everyone focuses on their OWN expectations and don't really bother to understand the expectations of the person they're dealing with. I've seen employees in a company who, when their boss approaches them with a particular problem, brush the problem off or say "this isn't part of my job description" or that "if you expect me to work past 5PM, then I expect a raise". Their attention is primarily focused on their own expectations, rather than on those of their boss. They will never make progress in their career. John is a friend of mine who would like to become an entrepreneur. Some months ago I called him and asked him if he was interested collaborating on a new business that we were launching in the marketing industry. He met me and one of my partners. We needed someone to look after the consulting projects our clients required. We would have trained him and, in the case that he achieved good results, which was very likely, we would have made him a partner. During the meeting John, instead of listening to what we needed (after all, we were the ones offering an opportunity), he told us in no uncertain terms what HE needed from us. The result: we chose someone else and now that area manages dozens of clients. John, not having focused on the expectations of others, remained invisible. What does your employer really need? If you're a business owner, what does your client really need? The companies that are most successful are those that try to look at things through the eyes of the customer, seeking to understand their needs and to invent new solutions to make their lives easier. You can try to tell me that these rules don't apply to you, that you don't own a business, but let me just say: you're still an entrepreneur. You are an entrepreneur of yourself, a micro business that interacts with a range of customers: your employer is a customer, your colleagues are your customers, and certainly the company's customers are customers to your own "micro-enterprise". What are their needs? Try for half an hour to observe life through their eyes. What worries them?

What causes them to lose time? What are they having trouble with? Just by answering these questions and doing what comes to mind, your value to the market, and consequently your monetary earnings, will increase drastically. Some argue that it's not that simple. That if we have a warehouse role and our employer's problem is in sales, then it's not up to us to solve it. That's exactly the mentality of 80% of the population living on 20% of the available wealth! The individual who, going against the trend, takes responsibility for the employer's problem regarding sales, will be the individual that the employer then considers to be of greater economic value. Others may argue that "no, that's not possible". Even if they did more, their boss would never reward their efforts. To this second group I answer that if they continue to work more than they are paid, inevitably they will end up being paid more than what they are paid now. It's just plain math. In my company the individual who is the highest paid of all is a guy who came to work here a few years ago. I still remember his first meeting with us: "Let's not talk about salary for now. Just tell me what you need from me, and then pay me based on what I do." And later, whenever a problem emerged in the company, he was the first to take responsibility, to say how it could be solved. Even though he took care of his own interests, he was not so single-minded that he renegotiated his salary every time we asked him to do something else. He ended up becoming indispensable. And if we had not 17 However, despite the many books on the subject, today almost everyone focuses on their OWN expectations and don't really bother to understand the expectations of the person they're dealing with. I've seen employees in a company who, when their boss approaches them with a particular problem, brush the problem off or say "this isn't part of my job description" or that "if you expect me to work past 5PM, then I expect a raise". Their attention is primarily focused on their own expectations, rather than on those of their boss. They will never make progress in their career. John is a friend of mine who would like to become an entrepreneur. Some months ago I called him and asked him if he was interested collaborating on a new business that we were launching in the marketing industry. He met me and one of my partners. We needed someone to look after the consulting projects our clients required. We would have trained him and, in the case that he achieved good results, which was very likely, we would have made him a partner. During the meeting John, instead of listening to what we needed (after all, we were the ones offering an opportunity), he told us in no uncertain terms what HE needed from us. The result: we chose someone else and now that area manages dozens of clients. John, not having focused on the expectations of others, remained invisible. What does your employer really need? If you're a business owner, what does your client really need? The companies that are most successful are those that try to look at things through the eyes of the customer, seeking to understand their needs and to invent new solutions to make their lives easier. You can try to tell me that these rules don't apply to you, that you don't own a business, but let me just say: you're still an entrepreneur. You are an entrepreneur of yourself, a micro business that interacts with a range of customers: your employer is a customer, your colleagues are your customers, and certainly the company's customers are customers to your own "micro-enterprise". What are their needs? Try for half an hour to observe life through their eyes. What worries them? What causes them to lose time? What are they having trouble with? Just by answering these questions and doing what comes to mind, your value to the market, and consequently your monetary earnings, will increase drastically. Some argue that it's not that simple. That if we have a warehouse role and our employer's problem is in sales, then it's not up to us to solve it. That's exactly the mentality of 80% of the population living on 20% of the available wealth! The individual who, going against the trend, takes responsibility for the employer's problem regarding sales, will be the individual that the employer then considers to be of greater economic value. Others may argue that "no, that's not possible". Even if they did more, their boss would never reward their efforts. To this second group I answer that if they continue to work more than they are paid, inevitably they will end up being paid more than what they are paid now. It's just plain math. In my company the individual who is the highest paid of all is a guy who came to work here a few years ago. I still remember his first meeting with us: "Let's not talk about salary for now. Just tell me what you need from me, and then pay me based on what I do." And later, whenever a problem emerged in the company, he was the first to take responsibility, to say how it could be solved. Even though he took care of his own interests, he was not so single-minded that he renegotiated his salary every time we asked him to do something else. He ended up becoming indispensable. And if we had not 18 paid him what he was worth, surely one of our customers or competitors, seeing the way he works, would be willing to do so. But that's not all. Exceed expectations: how to become indispensable "Exceed your customer's expectations. If you do, they'll come back over and over. Give them what they want - and a little more. " Sam Walton, founder of Walmart Sometimes in life we meet someone who exceeds our expectations. We take our car in for a tune up and not only did we get a good tune up for a decent price (our expectations), but the car was even washed for free. How do we react in those cases? We are amazed. The fact that someone has exceeded our expectations takes us by surprise and turns us into a walking advertisement for that person or firm. We speak well about that mechanic to anyone we meet, happily providing free advertising. Our promotion will bring more clients or, at least, guarantee our own loyalty. Whenever we have a small car problem, we will remember that mechanic. It works the same way in a company. The employee who exceeds the expectations of their boss will inevitably end up being involved in major projects, with more responsibility and, who knows, one day might even end up being partner in the same company for which they worked (this has happened more than once). Unfortunately this theory, which Napoleon Hill calls the theory of being willing to go the "extra mile", is not widespread in society. Instead, people have grown accustomed to only "getting what they paid for" or, in some cases, receiving even less than they expected. Meanwhile, the people who regularly endeavor to exceed the expectations of customers with whom they interact, inevitably become indispensable, a point of reference and standard baseline. Even little gestures will pay off big in the future. I understand that a business or individual can't simply "give away" their products or efforts. There must be some kind of exchange. I'm not saying that we should work for free or give discounts and extended payment terms. We have to charge the right price for what we do, but once we get into business with a customer we need to try to adhere to the philosophy of "going the extra mile": always giving more than the customer expects. This is literally the road to riches and opportunity. In my company, when I have a new important project, who do you think I'll assign it to? My lazy employee, who always brings up salary negotiations or working hours every time I ask for something, or the employee who, despite other flaws, always tries to give me more than what I expected? If you work more than what you're paid for, you will inevitably end up earning more than what you're paid now. 19 Let's be honest: if you're an employee who relies on an average salary with a raise every couple of years, you will never be rich nor wealthy. You will live life on the edge, making ends meet, and often having few financial resources. If you want to get out of this situation, you need to exceed the expectations of your boss or those who manage you. Doing more than what they expected. Exceed the expectations of your customers and continue to do so even if it seems that your efforts are not paying off. Fully adopt this rule for success. You'll see that even if some people don't seem to notice it, others surely will. Truly good employees aren't left underpaid for long. Some of us in the past have had a bad experience with someone they helped, or have given a lot without receiving anything in return. Some employees, when I explain this success rule, tell me that it doesn't work, they've already tried it and the other person not only didn't repay them, but even exploited it, and merely walked all over them. From this single failure they have deduced the wrong lesson: that exceeding the expectations of their client doesn't work. These people need to know two additional lessons about success: a) The market, at its core, has supreme justice. If you exceed the expectations of the customer as a general way of life, sooner or later the market will reward you. Perhaps that specific person won't reward you, but someone else will in some way. b) As we will see later in this book, you should not expect instant gratification on the path to success. Rather, you must have the courage to persist for months, sometimes years, in following the rules of success. A friend of mine was a teacher in a public school. The salary, as often indicated in the news and social media, was not very good. But he made a point of exceeding the expectations of others. So not only did he strive to be a good teacher by studying and staying up to date, often at his own expense, but was available for students or even parents to meet in the afternoon or even in the evenings. He had a passion for his subject, and also experimented with new methods of study and new programs. When he spoke with the parents of the students, he didn't just explain how their children were doing, but spent time listening and giving practical advice on how to help children grow and become capable in life. He was the first who offered to help when another teacher was ill, often working longer hours than he was actually paid for. Despite all of this, his salary did not increase. This went on for three years. Then one day a parent of one of his pupils, who happened to run a company, recognized his great potential, which no one else in the school had ever done up to that point. She asked him to become the head of training at her company. And so a normal teacher found himself becoming a very successful manager. Working more than he was paid, it was inevitable that he would end up earning more than he had in the past. The moral of this rule is simple: the market recognizes and rewards people who regularly strive to recognize and exceed the expectations of their clients. Sometimes it doesn't do so right away, you may feel like you're being exploited for a while, but in the long run, continuing to work more than you're paid, it is INEVITABLE that you will end up earning more. Forget about the individual cases in which you have given more without receiving anything in return, stop thinking only about your own expectations and focus on those of the person in front of you. Try to give them what they expect and... a little more. Not only will your 19 Let's be honest: if you're an employee who relies on an average salary with a raise every couple of years, you will never be rich nor wealthy. You will live life on the edge, making ends meet, and often having few financial resources. If you want to get out of this situation, you need to exceed the expectations of your boss or those who manage you. Doing more than what they expected. Exceed the expectations of your customers and continue to do so even if it seems that your efforts are not paying off. Fully adopt this rule for success. You'll see that even if some people don't seem to notice it, others surely will. Truly good employees aren't left underpaid for long. Some of us in the past have had a bad experience with someone they helped, or have given a lot without receiving anything in return. Some employees, when I explain this success rule, tell me that it doesn't work, they've already tried it and the other person not only didn't repay them, but even exploited it, and merely walked all over them. From this single failure they have deduced the wrong lesson: that exceeding the expectations of their client doesn't work. These people need to know two additional lessons about success: a) The market, at its core, has supreme justice. If you exceed the expectations of the customer as a general way of life, sooner or later the market will reward you. Perhaps that specific person won't reward you, but someone else will in some way. b) As we will see later in this book, you should not expect instant gratification on the path to success. Rather, you must have the courage to persist for months, sometimes years, in following the rules of success. A friend of mine was a teacher in a public school. The salary, as often indicated in the news and social media, was not very good. But he made a point of exceeding the expectations of others. So not only did he strive to be a good teacher by studying and staying up to date, often at his own expense, but was available for students or even parents to meet in the afternoon or even in the evenings. He had a passion for his subject, and also experimented with new methods of study and new programs. When he spoke with the parents of the students, he didn't just explain how their children were doing, but spent time listening and giving practical advice on how to help children grow and become capable in life. He was the first who offered to help when another teacher was ill, often working longer hours than he was actually paid for. Despite all of this, his salary did not increase. This went on for three years. Then one day a parent of one of his pupils, who happened to run a company, recognized his great potential, which no one else in the school had ever done up to that point. She asked him to become the head of training at her company. And so a normal teacher found himself becoming a very successful manager. Working more than he was paid, it was inevitable that he would end up earning more than he had in the past. The moral of this rule is simple: the market recognizes and rewards people who regularly strive to recognize and exceed the expectations of their clients. Sometimes it doesn't do so right away, you may feel like you're being exploited for a while, but in the long run, continuing to work more than you're paid, it is INEVITABLE that you will end up earning more. Forget about the individual cases in which you have given more without receiving anything in return, stop thinking only about your own expectations and focus on those of the person in front of you. Try to give them what they expect and... a little more. Not only will your 20 income increase, but magically YOU WILL FIND YOURSELF IN A POSITION WHERE YOU ARE NOTICED AND GET OPPORTUNITIES. Why continue to suffer, blind to the many opportunities that surround us, just because some episodes of our lives have crippled our TRUE personality and convinced us that it is not worth understanding and exceeding the expectations of others? If you understand the expectations of others, others will be more willing to understand and be interested in yours. Give it a try!

CHAPTER FOUR

Become a great human being!

I would like you to think for a moment, what it means to be a "great human being". It's not about being beautiful, famous, or a hero. It's simply being the kind of person who makes others say "Wow, what a great person. I'm so happy I met them." Someone who puts you at ease, makes you feel good deep down inside yourself, who truly believes in the values they promote, who not only talks the talk but also walks the walk, a person you can trust. Success requires you to become this kind of person. If you do not, success, as well as money, will always be out of reach. And any success or wealth you do manage to grasp will only be temporary and will slip away as quickly as it came. This rule is in sharp contrast to the stereotype of the successful person: someone who is always surrounded by bodyguards, difficult to approach, a lone wolf or shark, or in some cases a grim dictator. All these are nonsense stereotypes, and in this chapter we'll see why. The value of alliances In my first book, The New Leaders2, I mention an aspect of successful people that is often neglected. The individual, the lone wolf, does not have success, they merely survive. We are sometimes misled by the fact that we see leaders climbing into the limelight who are presented as divine figures, someone who started with nothing and single-handedly built a great empire. In reality, a successful person needs a group of allies. Often this group of allies is in the form of partners or trusted associates, other times it takes the form of clients with whom our successful person has "conspired" for a long time, making plans and projects. Often these allies are in the shadows, and accept that the leader alone will be the one to enjoy the limelight, but they nevertheless play a crucial role in the materialization of the leader's success. Elon Musk appears to be a person who has achieved success alone, when in fact his success has been greatly helped by his original partners, not to mention the numerous technicians, suppliers and employees that Musk managed to win over the years. Tesla is now in high demand all over the world not only because of its quality as a car, but also because Musk was able to build the best network of alliances possible. Consider any product that is now established in the market. Do you really think that only its innovation and quality is what allowed it to become a leading product? Or large sums of company money that put it on the market? Of course these things certainly help, but without the network of alliances created by the founder of that company, the product would not be where it is today. Brian Tracy says that "A person will not buy from you until he is convinced that you are a friend and are acting in his best interest." Variations of this law are often repeated by anyone who has written about sales: from Zig Ziglar to Og Mandino. The network of alliances built by a company is often more valuable than any building or product. Your ability to succeed depends, in no small part, on how big your network of alliances is. This network of alliances can do much, much more for you than any financial investment. It will be this network of alliances that supports you, which will offer you opportunities, will comfort you or motivate you when things go wrong, will help promote your products if you should decide to become an entrepreneur. The network of alliances is not just a quantitative concept, but also qualitative. The more skilled and powerful the people in it are, the greater your chances of success, if only for the fact that having such people in your network gives you access to better advice. James is a consultant in my company. He's a hard worker, perhaps the hardest working person I know, often working through the weekends. He is faithful, loyal, and technically skilled. In short, he is the type of employee that every good manager would like to have. However, despite all of his positive qualities, Jamie has struggled to prosper within our company. His shortcoming: he is unable to create a network of alliances. When visiting a client company if someone disagrees with him, he tends to clash with them, perceiving them as a rival, a competitor, someone who does not accept his "beliefs". And, inevitably, it climaxes in a duel to the death. Sometimes he wins and manages to impose his ideas on others and keeping the customer, sometimes he loses, and with it his influence on the customer. By operating in this way he is never able to build a network of stable customers, to say nothing of coworkers. Rather than trying to help them win, James tries to make them accept his point of view, his way of working and, as soon as any of them do not work as he would like, he inevitably marginalizes. Although perhaps the best within our structure as regards dedication, technical expertise and work ethic,

James never manages to have a stable network of alliances that facilitates success. By contrast, a few weeks ago I interviewed Eusebio, a dear friend and CEO of a leading company in the bathroom furnishing industry. What most strikes me about Eusebio is his ability to maintain excellent relations with everyone he has ever met. This ability has helped him greatly to build a very successful company from nothing. His point of view surprised me because it goes against the mentality of many other managers (managers who, I might add, are doing quite poorly): "I have no hostility towards anyone. I find it difficult to dislike someone, even if they have wronged me. For many years I've been considered strange because I've never been able to engage in conflict. Even if someone has done something bad, I could never just cut them off without another word." Discovering his secret has helped me a lot to also understand the one key reason behind success: Eusebio has and maintains an attractive personality. This has allowed him to build a network of alliances throughout the world. A network of alliances is worth much more than all the money you have in the bank. The reason is simple: if you have a lot of money, but no alliances, sooner or later the money will dry up (unless you really have an absurd amount of money already). If you don't have money, but you have alliances, then it will be possible to build your wealth. A great human being A great human being is someone other people want to be around, someone with whom others want to do business, someone who makes you feel good. Sometimes we believe, erroneously, that an "attractive personality" is someone who knows how to entertain others, someone brilliant with a ready wit, who monopolizes the conversations, and leaves us shyly thinking we could never be as cool as them. In reality this is not so. 23 An attractive person, a "great human being", is not about being a stand-up comedian, or being the person with the most exotic travel story. Instead, it is a personality composed of certain qualities that anyone can develop: 1) A great human being puts others, and the needs of others, at the center of the conversation. Today, when people speak, they will often tell you all about their ideas and their stories. There are very few however, who can put others at the center of the conversation. According to Zig Ziglar, a master in sales, a good salesperson does not convince people by talking, but by asking questions. Ziglar, as well as many other researchers, say that to convince someone of something you must first listen to them. If you do not listen or aren't really interested in them, then they will never be interested in you or your product. If you are shy, this is no problem. In fact, in order to develop an attractive personality it is better if you don't talk much, but instead listen to others and be interested in them. It's about being curious and fascinated by the stories of other people. If you can show curiosity or interest in a person, asking questions and listening to what they say for at least 15 minutes, a fascinating psychological phenomenon occurs: they will consider you an expert in the field even if you haven't said a single word. Even before the times of Christ, Publilius Syrus said: "We are interested in others only when they are interested in us." Even Adler mentions people who fail to be interested in others, insisting that "These are the people who fail in their intent." Be interested in the people around you, try to find out about their story, how things are at home, what they do with their children, how they got started at their current job. In the end, not only will you earn more, but I assure you that it will add a much more entertaining and gratifying depth to your life. However, being interested is not just about listening or acting curious. Showing interest means forgetting about what YOU need for a while, and instead talking first and foremost about what OTHERS feel or need. If you can do this, you'll see that you will always be better appreciated as well as better paid. I believe that the most beautiful words we can say to a person are: "How can I help you?" 2) A great human being is empathetic. Empathy means being able to feel what others feel. Our actions and our words always have an effect of some kind on others. Every single day. If you've never noticed this, make sure to take a closer look. What we say can disappoint the expectations of others, it can strengthen their dreams or projects, inspire others or throw them into despair. People are often proud and will not want to confess this, but what you say can sometimes create devastating emotional effects. Strive to observe others and TAKE RESPONSIBILITY FOR WHAT OTHERS FEEL! If they are sad, pick them up in good spirits. If they are worried, give them encouragement. If they are agitated, listen to them and try to help them find a solution. You will make plenty of 23 An attractive person, a "great human being", is not about being a stand-up comedian, or being the person with the most exotic travel story. Instead, it is a personality composed of certain qualities that anyone can develop: 1) A great human being puts others, and the needs of others, at the center of the conversation. Today, when people speak, they will often tell you all about their ideas and their stories. There are very few however, who can put others at the center of the conversation. According to Zig Ziglar, a master in sales, a good salesperson does not convince people by talking, but by asking questions. Ziglar, as well as many other researchers, say that to convince someone of something you must first listen to them. If you do not listen or aren't really interested in them, then they will never be interested in you or your product. If you are shy, this is no problem. In fact, in order to develop an attractive personality it is better if you don't talk much, but instead listen to others and be interested in them. It's about being curious and fascinated by the stories of other people. If you can show curiosity or interest in a person, asking questions and listening to what they say for at least 15 minutes, a fascinating psychological phenomenon occurs: they will consider you an expert in the field even if you haven't said a single word. Even before the times of Christ, Publilius Syrus said: "We are interested in others only when they are interested in us." Even Adler mentions people who fail to be interested in others, insisting that "These are the people who fail in their intent." Be interested in the people around you, try to find out about their story, how things are at home, what they do with their children, how they got started at their current job. In the end, not only will you earn more, but I assure you that it will add a much more entertaining and gratifying depth to your life. However, being interested is not just about listening or acting curious. Showing interest means forgetting about what YOU need for a while, and instead talking first and foremost about what OTHERS feel or need. If you can do this, you'll see that you will always be better appreciated as well as better paid. I believe that the most beautiful words we can say to a person are: "How can I help you?" 2) A great human being is empathetic. Empathy means being able to feel what others feel. Our actions and our words always have an effect of some kind on others. Every single day. If you've never noticed this, make sure to take a closer look. What we say can disappoint the expectations of others, it can strengthen their dreams or projects, inspire others or throw them into despair. People are often proud and will not want to confess this, but what you say can sometimes create devastating emotional effects. Strive to observe others and TAKE RESPONSIBILITY FOR WHAT OTHERS FEEL! If they are sad, pick them up in good spirits. If they are worried, give them encouragement. If they are agitated, listen to them and try to help them find a solution. You will make plenty of 24 mistakes, but still try to do something for them. By simply doing this, you will not only create many true friends, but your income will also begin to increase. Part of empathy includes being guided by a sense of justice. Remember to be fair, to protect the weak, to fight against abuses. Do it effectively, do not limit yourself to merely expressing your sympathy or being sad with them. It does not necessarily pay off in economic terms, but the gratification that ensues will make you feel good about yourself and will put you in the emotional condition necessary to work well. 3) A great human being is humble. If you know someone who has truly achieved success, you will have noticed that they are humble people, who do not show off their skills or their excellence. When someone tells them that they have done well, the true leaders will always say something like "my coworkers were the ones who did the real work, I just helped them coordinate." Maradona (one of the greatest soccer players of all time), after making an extraordinary goal, would always say: "It wasn't me, it was the team". And when it was obvious that the merit was his because he had single handedly maneuvered the entire the length of the field, responded to praise by saying: "I got lucky". It is not that you have to forget about your skills. If you stop respecting yourself it will be the end of you, just don't talk about it in front of others. Never differentiate yourself from others according to what you possess or have. When someone introduces me to a client by saying that I am the CEO of Open Source Management, the one who wrote The New Leaders, the one that trained all the consultants, I always reply in kind by pointing out that I am also "the one that spends Saturday morning cleaning the office bathrooms if clients are visiting that day, to make sure we give a good impression." If you're dealing with someone who obviously has a lot less than you or who obviously lacks skills compared to you, respect them and treat them well, talk to them as if they were your equal. Be nice to the waiters at restaurants, hostesses or check-in clerks at airports. You'll be surprised how rewarding this is for you and, above all, for them. 4) A great human being doesn't take things too seriously. Dawn is a friend of mine who works as an HR Manager. Things are never a problem with her, because she plays down any difficulties she encounters. Perhaps it is this quality that has made her one of the highest paid and appreciated people in her company. If there is any trouble, while everyone else is sucked into a black hole of despair, Dawn tries to find a way to joke about it. If a colleague isn't working well, rather than bluntly demanding answers, she confronts the person with the help of a few jokes about the incident. She is the best personnel manager I've ever met. Playing down problems or joking always brings out the best in other people and puts them at ease, as opposed to many other managers I know who always "want to get to the bottom of the problem and highlight all the disciplinary shortcomings". 25 At first glance, some would say this kind of person isn't serious enough, that their tendency to joke is harmful because laughter is distracting. But, in reality, their humor is regenerating people and actually dramatically increases productivity. A "serious personality", which focuses on the dark side of every problem, is very formal, with a tendency for disciplinary proceedings, is perhaps the worst misfortune that can befall a person. Stop taking yourself so seriously. If you know any successful people, then you know that they are all happy people, who put you at ease and like to joke. If you're dealing with people who are too earnest, abandon them because they will be your downfall. 5) A great human being is inspired by a goal. It is very clear on where it is going. Up until now, it seems as if a great human being is simply someone who gets along with everyone, is good with everyone, and knows how to put everyone at ease... but this is not enough. Great human beings are committed, in the sense that they know where they're headed. A great human being is not a loser, but someone who believes in something, who has some project that fascinates and excites them. If you do not pursue a goal, no matter how good you are with people, others will not respect you, because deep down they see you as a person who isn't going anywhere in life. You'll never become a model, and you'll never become a point of reference. If you still haven't done so, establish a goal or set of goals, ones that are achievable but also challenging, and, as an entrepreneur friend of mine says, plow ahead without stopping for anything. It is my firm belief that the majority of people in society merely "survive" without ever going anywhere. A part of this unfortunate majority are those who attempt to break through in some area, but as soon as they are faced with the first difficulties they abandon it. The person who persists however, even if things aren't going so well in the beginning, but still hold on, soon earns the respect of those who didn't get anywhere or gave up too quickly. And the latter, inevitably, will become part of their sphere of influence and network of alliances. 6) A great human being has a high sense of ethics. Being ethical mainly means keeping true to your word, no deviation from the agreements made, don't treat others in a way that you wouldn't want to be treated. Today, there are depressingly few people in society with a high sense of personal ethics. The average person thinks that if they cheat, if they benefit unfairly by taking advantage of others, that they're not really doing anything wrong. Instead they call themselves "crafty", "cunning", or "savvy". I hate to say something that clearly goes against the trend, but without a doubt I have found that the people who regularly commit actions that must then be hidden or "covered up", don't get anywhere in the long run. 25 At first glance, some would say this kind of person isn't serious enough, that their tendency to joke is harmful because laughter is distracting. But, in reality, their humor is regenerating people and actually dramatically increases productivity. A "serious personality", which focuses on the dark side of every problem, is very formal, with a tendency for disciplinary proceedings, is perhaps the worst misfortune that can befall a person. Stop taking yourself so seriously. If you know any successful people, then you know that they are all happy people, who put you at ease and like to joke. If you're dealing with people who are too earnest, abandon them because they will be your downfall. 5) A great human being is inspired by a goal. It is very clear on where it is going. Up until now, it seems as if a great human being is simply someone who gets along with everyone, is good with everyone, and knows how to put everyone at ease... but this is not enough. Great human beings are committed, in the sense that they know where they're headed. A great human being is not a loser, but someone who believes in something, who has some project that fascinates and excites them. If you do not pursue a goal, no matter how good you are with people, others will not respect you, because deep down they see you as a person who isn't going anywhere in life. You'll never become a model, and you'll never become a point of reference. If you still haven't done so, establish a goal or set of goals, ones that are achievable but also challenging, and, as an entrepreneur friend of mine says, plow ahead without stopping for anything. It is my firm belief that the majority of people in society merely "survive" without ever going anywhere. A part of this unfortunate majority are those who attempt to break through in some area, but as soon as they are faced with the first difficulties they abandon it. The person who persists however, even if things aren't going so well in the beginning, but still hold on, soon earns the respect of those who didn't get anywhere or gave up too quickly. And the latter, inevitably, will become part of their sphere of influence and network of alliances. 6) A great human being has a high sense of ethics. Being ethical mainly means keeping true to your word, no deviation from the agreements made, don't treat others in a way that you wouldn't want to be treated. Today, there are depressingly few people in society with a high sense of personal ethics. The average person thinks that if they cheat, if they benefit unfairly by taking advantage of others, that they're not really doing anything wrong. Instead they call themselves "crafty", "cunning", or "savvy". I hate to say something that clearly goes against the trend, but without a doubt I have found that the people who regularly commit actions that must then be hidden or "covered up", don't get anywhere in the long run. 26 Life is a set of communicating vessels. You cannot commit detrimental or unethical actions in one area of your life, for example in the family sphere, without allowing these acts to also cause negative consequences in all other areas of your life. The cheating spouse, the warehouse employee who steals, the salesperson who abuses company expense reimbursement, the business owner who uses methods that skirt the edge of the law... these people may call themselves "crafty", but they are also people who, without realizing it, have tangled their lives in a way that will eventually make them ineffective. If you look at things objectively and think of the areas where you're keeping secrets, or did things that you would rather hide, you will realize that these are also the areas where you are the least effective, where you have to "put up with" other people, and where you are most anxious. Transgressions can sometimes be a source of pleasure, but you should know that when you break certain rules or do something that you would not want other people to know about, it's like you are writing a check. Even if what you did will never be found out, sooner or later that check will be cashed, meaning that you will pay the consequences. You become anxious and ineffective, your life becomes chaotic, and it not only affects the area where you transgressed, but bit by bit, like a drop of ink that has been put into a set of connected vessels, it will expand throughout your life making you less effective everywhere. When you are involved in unethical activities, it feels like the whole world is "conspiring" against you. 7) A great human being is reliable and does what it promises. Being reliable means becoming a person whom others can trust. If you say you will do something, do it. If you do not keep your promises, or do not respect agreements, you become unreliable (in the sense that people cannot rely on you) and people will flee from your network of alliances like it's a sinking ship. That's why ethics are so important. That's why keeping one's word is so important. True, maintaining certain commitments can sometimes cost you time and effort, but every time you do, your value in the market increases. One of the things that has contributed most to the growth of my company is the policy of "if we made a promise to a customer, we have to keep it even if it costs more than what they pay us." Not only has this policy saved us from ruin, but it has also allowed us to create a prosperous and respected business. Being reliable sometimes also requires good personal organization. Learn the habit of writing what you need to do every day. If you talk with someone, take notes. Once every two or three weeks re-read these notes, review your work plans and take note of anything that still isn't done. If you do this well, other people will always be surprised at your ability to maintain control of situations. 8) A great human being is not afraid to openly declare its own faults. If you want to succeed you must have the courage to not take yourself too seriously. The best people in the world are those who embrace self-irony. They have the courage to joke about themselves. This, contrary to what one might think, is not a sign of weakness, but a sign of strength. 27 The most difficult employees you have to deal with are the touchy ones. Show them something they can improve on and they will either be blatantly offended, or sulk and give you the silent treatment. They take it personally. Then you have to motivate them again, energize them, get them talking. After you dealt with them you find yourself thinking about how to make sure the most important projects are directed towards other people: people with self-irony, who don't get offended when you show them what they can improve. But before looking at your colleagues or employees, take a good look at yourself: are you brave enough to make fun of yourself? Are you able to joke about your weaknesses? Or do you hide behind a mountain of excuses every time something is pointed out to you, insisting that you are right? Or, even worse, do you get offended? If this is how you act, then people will stop involving you in their projects and stop offering you opportunities, now that they know what you're like. The ability to accept criticism and self-improvement is a key feature not only for success, but also (and most importantly) for simply being a part of the world. A great human being, in any interaction, will always think about what's good FOR YOU in that interaction. Yes, that's right. A great human being looks for the win-win. In any activity they not only try to win for themselves, but also to win for you. And not just with words in order to get you to swallow the pill and accept the deal, but really and truly win. This is how you earn the respect, goodwill, and cooperation of others. I know some managers who are exceptionally determined negotiators, in the sense that aim for the best price with the best conditions, and rightly so. Sometimes price lists are inflated and simply asking certainly can't hurt, but it shouldn't be done excessively, such as to the point of creating a win-lose situation (where you win but the other person loses). If you push it to this point, then the next time this vendor has to deal with you they will hardly be willing to help you out, and rest assured that they will not speak well of you. By winning money for your partners, your employer, your colleagues, and your friends, you are simultaneously earning something for yourself that is much more valuable than any money you may have spent: a network of alliances that, in the future, will be of great help in earning you a lot of money. My company's motto has always been this: if we help our employees earn well, surely we ourselves will gain immeasurably more. That's how we were able to build a leading and respected company, starting from nothing and with no money. Be generous, think win-win, think about how to make money for the people who are in business with you, be they clients, employers or employees. Work to earn money for yourself, but remember to make money for your peers as well. Become a great human being Our actions determine who we are. No matter what kind of character or personality you have at this time. If you train yourself to act with the characteristics of an attractive personality, you will inevitably become that person. To the extent that by adopting this personality, your network of alliances will strengthen and expand. To the extent that by strengthening and expanding your network of alliances, your prosperity and success will also increase. It is helpful at this time to take a sheet of paper and do a self-evaluation regarding the characteristics of a great human being. Examine the qualities described in this chapter one by one and make an analysis of yourself. 1) Which characteristics would you like to improve? 2) What practical actions can you take in the coming weeks to make these qualities a part of the way you normally act? Write real practical actions, for each characteristic. If you do, I assure you that in the coming days and weeks, you will make great strides towards success. Remember, we become what we do. The actions and methods that we choose to adopt in every hour, every day, and every week will determine, more than anything else will, the direction of your path on the road success or failure. You're the one behind the wheel. Become a great human being!

CHAPTER FIVE

The turning point

The regular application of the first four rules will remove you from the condition of invisibility. You'll be surprised when you realize exactly how many opportunities you already have around you. Upon seeing your predisposition to go the "extra mile" and to meet and exceed the expectations of others, people will start to involve you more and more in their projects. By becoming a better person, your network of alliances will begin to grow and you'll find yourself entertaining evermore important and fruitful relationships. What is more, however strange it may seem, the fact of applying the first four rules of success will not only bring you the aforementioned advantages, but it will also bring you to what I call the TURNING POINT. This is a phase of your business or personal life that you will sooner or later be forced to face and overcome. If you remain invisible, nothing dramatic will happen. Meaning that you won't get anywhere, you won't build anything important, and things will simply continue to be "sort of ok". If, however, you decide to apply the first four rules of success, you will be launched out of invisibility and find yourself face to face with the Turning Point. The Turning Point can be identified as the central phase located between invisibility and the materialization of success, as shown in the diagram below: INVISIBILITY (No opportunities, or an inability to recognize real opportunities. Mere survival. Chasing mirages rather than opportunities) ? VISIBILITY (Becoming involved in opportunities. Life improves) ? TURNING POINT ? TRUE MATERIALIZATION OF SUCCESS The Turning Point is a crucial moment on the road to success. By overcoming it you will be able to proceed to the materialization of real success. Most people never get to materialize success precisely because they get hung up at this point. ? Application of the first 4 rules of success.

The Turning Point generally manifests when either your personal or professional life stops going well. Someone who has realized that they should apply the first four rules, will at first see their life or business improve and step out of invisibility, only to bump into this wall. Generally, at this point, they become confused: deep down they know they are doing the right things (becoming a professional at what they do, working hard, meeting and exceeding the expectations of others and trying to act like a great human being). But then they stumble through a whole series of new phenomena that discourages them: their sphere of influence has now grown, causing them to feel more stressed out, running into new problems, sometimes having ups and downs. There are two solutions available to someone at this turning point: a) become discouraged and go back into invisibility b) hold on and try, by working even harder, to achieve success. Solution a), as you can understand, isn't really a solution. Those who choose solution a) fall into the trap explained in the first rule: thinking that success is only achievable by finding "the right opportunity" or "getting lucky". They have already tried the first four rules, but apparently they did not get to enjoy any of the benefits. So back to chasing red herrings. Solution b) is the reason why those who are at the top of a company often appear to be stressed out. Our own aptitude analysis, which we conducted on over 250,000 entrepreneurs and professionals, has shown that despite having reached important economic objectives, these people are agitated, stressed and worried. The primary reason for what is commonly known as "success stress", which afflicts so many managers and celebrities, is perhaps the fact that the Turning Point has been surpassed only by sheer physical strength and hard work, rather than making some practical changes in their own lives, as we shall see in the fifth, sixth, and seventh rules. So let's take a closer look at why the "infamous" Turning Point manifests in this way. The Turning Point If you follow rules 1-4 diligently, you will escape from invisibility. The more visible you become though, however good that is, it also brings its own problem: now people can see you. And they will not only see your desire to work and to succeed, but will also notice a number of shortcomings that you've been carrying around for a long time. These defects, which all of us have, were probably just small shortcomings up until yesterday, but now that your sphere of influence has increased, it's as if everything is under a magnifying glass. While these defects were not an issue for someone who was part of the 80% of the population living on just 20% of the wealth, they are certainly a problem for someone who has started to get involved in important opportunities. There are two responses to your flaws: either they point them out to you constantly and complain about it, causing you frustration, lack of motivation, and in some cases drastically increasing your stress. Or they sneak away and stop involving you. They saw you as a promising person, but looking more closely they realized that you weren't really as good or reliable as they had thought. These defects or shortcomings are not only a problem for the people we interact with. They are primarily a problem for you. Now that you have applied the first four rules and your sphere of influence has expanded, you must quickly do something to manage these 31 The Turning Point generally manifests when either your personal or professional life stops going well. Someone who has realized that they should apply the first four rules, will at first see their life or business improve and step out of invisibility, only to bump into this wall. Generally, at this point, they become confused: deep down they know they are doing the right things (becoming a professional at what they do, working hard, meeting and exceeding the expectations of others and trying to act like a great human being). But then they stumble through a whole series of new phenomena that discourages them: their sphere of influence has now grown, causing them to feel more stressed out, running into new problems, sometimes having ups and downs. There are two solutions available to someone at this turning point: a) become discouraged and go back into invisibility b) hold on and try, by working even harder, to achieve success. Solution a), as you can understand, isn't really a solution. Those who choose solution a) fall into the trap explained in the first rule: thinking that success is only achievable by finding "the right opportunity" or "getting lucky". They have already tried the first four rules, but apparently they did not get to enjoy any of the benefits. So back to chasing red herrings. Solution b) is the reason why those who are at the top of a company often appear to be stressed out. Our own aptitude analysis, which we conducted on over 250,000 entrepreneurs and professionals, has shown that despite having reached important economic objectives, these people are agitated, stressed and worried. The primary reason for what is commonly known as "success stress", which afflicts so many managers and celebrities, is perhaps the fact that the Turning Point has been surpassed only by sheer physical strength and hard work, rather than making some practical changes in their own lives, as we shall see in the fifth, sixth, and seventh rules. So let's take a closer look at why the "infamous" Turning Point manifests in this way. The Turning Point If you follow rules 1-4 diligently, you will escape from invisibility. The more visible you become though, however good that is, it also brings its own problem: now people can see you. And they will not only see your desire to work and to succeed, but will also notice a number of shortcomings that you've been carrying around for a long time. These defects, which all of us have, were probably just small shortcomings up until yesterday, but now that your sphere of influence has increased, it's as if everything is under a magnifying glass. While these defects were not an issue for someone who was part of the 80% of the population living on just 20% of the wealth, they are certainly a problem for someone who has started to get involved in important opportunities. There are two responses to your flaws: either they point them out to you constantly and complain about it, causing you frustration, lack of motivation, and in some cases drastically increasing your stress. Or they sneak away and stop involving you. They saw you as a promising person, but looking more closely they realized that you weren't really as good or reliable as they had thought. These defects or shortcomings are not only a problem for the people we interact with. They are primarily a problem for you. Now that you have applied the first four rules and your sphere of influence has expanded, you must quickly do something to manage these 32 weaknesses. Otherwise they will transform from the small shortcomings of yesterday into veritable chasms that will trap you, fill your life with stress, and make it impossible for you to develop additional skills to help you materializing your success. You have arrived, in other words, at a crucial point. At this point you can either push ahead, or turn back. To survive the Turning Point you must have the courage to make some changes. Rules five, six, and seven will help you do that.

CHAPTER SIX

If you want things to change, first you have to change yourself

Those things that, up until just yesterday when you were still invisible, were small shortcomings, are now under a magnifying glass. If you reach the Turning Point and fail to confront and remove them, they will become chasms of weakness and stick a spoke in your wheel. People who have decided to be part of your network of alliances or who are offering you opportunities will notice and, if you don't change things, they will either hound you to the point of stress, or simply abandon you. If you do not do something to manage this, you will not survive the Turning Point. Instead, you will stop growing and fall back into invisibility. Alternatively, if you decide to grit your teeth and muscle your way through it to success, it will become a self-defeating exercise due to the exorbitant price you end up paying: your serenity and your happiness. These weaknesses typically appear in two ways. Some are personal: your own private shortcomings, weaknesses of character, attitudes and viewpoints that are not optimal. Then there are those that derive from the relationships you have with other people. We will discuss those last ones in rules 6 & 7. Change Are there unfriendly people working against you? The answer is yes, at least in one case. That person is you. Yesterday your weaknesses were so insignificant, with your smaller network of alliances, just one in the anonymous crowd of the 80% that gets nowhere. But now those weaknesses are in the spotlight, and you see that part of yourself is not optimal. The capable people who would like to join your network of alliances have probably already noticed these parts of you. They have eagle eyes, and if they share what they see with you, you can count yourself as lucky. Because very often they won't say a word to you, but they will certainly talk about it with each other. These small weaknesses were probably negligible before, but now they trip you up. You probably already know which weaknesses I'm talking about. Deep down there are things that you know, that perhaps someone has already pointed out to you in the past. They are those things that you have justified and justified until you start to believe that they aren't really weaknesses at all. They are those things that you criticize in others but don't acknowledge in yourself. The inabilities or handicaps that you turn a blind eye to. The bad habits, the goals that go against what you say. I'm sure you don't need anymore examples. You know what I'm talking about. 33 RULE 5 If you want things to change, first you have to change yourself Those things that, up until just yesterday when you were still invisible, were small shortcomings, are now under a magnifying glass. If you reach the Turning Point and fail to confront and remove them, they will become chasms of weakness and stick a spoke in your wheel. People who have decided to be part of your network of alliances or who are offering you opportunities will notice and, if you don't change things, they will either hound you to the point of stress, or simply abandon you. If you do not do something to manage this, you will not survive the Turning Point. Instead, you will stop growing and fall back into invisibility. Alternatively, if you decide to grit your teeth and muscle your way through it to success, it will become a self-defeating exercise due to the exorbitant price you end up paying: your serenity and your happiness. These weaknesses typically appear in two ways. Some are personal: your own private shortcomings, weaknesses of character, attitudes and viewpoints that are not optimal. Then there are those that derive from the relationships you have with other people. We will discuss those last ones in rules 6 & 7. Change Are there unfriendly people working against you? The answer is yes, at least in one case. That person is you. Yesterday your weaknesses were so insignificant, with your smaller network of alliances, just one in the anonymous crowd of the 80% that gets nowhere. But now those weaknesses are in the spotlight, and you see that part of yourself is not optimal. The capable people who would like to join your network of alliances have probably already noticed these parts of you. They have eagle eyes, and if they share what they see with you, you can count yourself as lucky. Because very often they won't say a word to you, but they will certainly talk about it with each other. These small weaknesses were probably negligible before, but now they trip you up. You probably already know which weaknesses I'm talking about. Deep down there are things that you know, that perhaps someone has already pointed out to you in the past. They are those things that you have justified and justified until you start to believe that they aren't really weaknesses at all. They are those things that you criticize in others but don't acknowledge in yourself. The inabilities or handicaps that you turn a blind eye to. The bad habits, the goals that go against what you say. I'm sure you don't need anymore examples. You know what I'm talking about. 34 In this chapter, you must have the courage to become a new person. Because, dear friend, if you do not change yourself, if you do not manage those things inside of you that you already know about, everything will just go right back to the way it was before. You may be wondering how I could possibly know this about you. There's no need to be too impressed. I have simply already been through all of this myself. I understand what you're going through, what you're experiencing. Knowing you as well as I do, let me say: it is time to become a new person! Continue to be a great human being In the fourth rule we described the characteristics of a great human being and we saw how reliability, empathy, and a win-win approach are important in creating a network of alliances. The moment your sphere of influence begins to grow though, all your weaknesses, even the smallest, come to light and make it more and more difficult for you to continue being a great human being and maintain the proper level of exchange with others. They keep you from being reliable. Indeed, how can you be considered reliable, if you're not even able to keep yourself organized? How can you be trusted, if you're secretly involved in activities that you hope no one will discover? How can you maintain a good quality of exchange, when your tendency to "just do everything yourself" makes it difficult for you to respect the agreed on timing? They prevent you from maintaining your sensitivity and empathy. How can you be considered caring if you're constantly grumpy or touchy? How can you possibly convince someone else that you're empathetic if, deep down, you don't really care about them? They prevent you from using a win-win mentality. How can you possibly maintain a winwin mentality (helping others to win) if, due to lack of expertise or knowledge about the new challenges presented in our work, we think we already have plenty of our own problems to deal with? If you do not manage your weaknesses (weaknesses, I repeat, that you yourself are very aware of), there will be a stampede as people flee your network of alliances. If you want things to change, first you have to change yourself Whatever difficulties you're experiencing right now, you should know that if you want things to change, you must first change yourself. Otherwise everything else you do will come to nothing. At this time in your life there may be people and situations that are disappointing you or with which you disagree. I ask you to please, for a moment, stop thinking about them. Stop thinking about the injustices you are suffering through, or all the wrongs other people are doing you. Let it go. First, we have to deal with you. 35 If we don't deal with ourselves, we'll never be able to deal successfully with the other people with whom we interact. Start with yourself first. If you don't change yourself, other people will never change, and you will never make it past the Turning Point. Lets do an exercise to examine your conduct, your character and the expectations that others have of you. In this exercise, I will need your full cooperation. It is a crucial step to overcome the turning point, so please pay close attention and do as I ask. If you struggle with this, at the end of the exercise I have put a box with an example showing how it's done. For the exercise you will need a pen, a sheet of paper, and 10 minutes of time in which you will not be disturbed. Get your pen and sheet of paper. Take a moment to look at things from the perspective of the people you interact with: your colleagues, your friends, your employees, your customers, your spouse, your children... in short, all the people you deal with every day. For a moment put your own thoughts aside, and look at yourself through their eyes. Then write out answers to these questions (answer only those that apply): 1a) What kind of (your name) does your spouse or partner expect? Describe. 1b) What secret or hidden trait in your behavior conflicts with the above? 2a) What kind of (your name) do the customers of your company expect? Describe. 2b) What secret or hidden trait in your behavior conflicts with the above? 3a) What kind of (your name) do your employees expect? Describe. 3b) What secret or hidden trait in your behavior conflicts with the above? 4a) What kind of (your name) does your boss or employer expect? Describe. 4b) What secret or hidden trait in your behavior conflicts with the above? 5a) What kind of (your name) do your colleagues, associates, or business partners expect? Describe. 5b) What secret or hidden trait in your behavior conflicts with the above? 6a) What kind of (your name) does society expect? Describe. 6b) What secret or hidden trait in your behavior conflicts with the above? 35 If we don't deal with ourselves, we'll never be able to deal successfully with the other people with whom we interact. Start with yourself first. If you don't change yourself, other people will never change, and you will never make it past the Turning Point. Lets do an exercise to examine your conduct, your character and the expectations that others have of you. In this exercise, I will need your full cooperation. It is a crucial step to overcome the turning point, so please pay close attention and do as I ask. If you struggle with this, at the end of the exercise I have put a box with an example showing how it's done. For the exercise you will need a pen, a sheet of paper, and 10 minutes of time in which you will not be disturbed. Get your pen and sheet of paper. Take a moment to look at things from the perspective of the people you interact with: your colleagues, your friends, your employees, your customers, your spouse, your children... in short, all the people you deal with every day. For a moment put your own thoughts aside, and look at yourself through their eyes. Then write out answers to these questions (answer only those that apply): 1a) What kind of (your name) does your spouse or partner expect? Describe. 1b) What secret or hidden trait in your behavior conflicts with the above? 2a) What kind of (your name) do the customers of your company expect? Describe. 2b) What secret or hidden trait in your behavior conflicts with the above? 3a) What kind of (your name) do your employees expect? Describe. 3b) What secret or hidden trait in your behavior conflicts with the above? 4a) What kind of (your name) does your boss or employer expect? Describe. 4b) What secret or hidden trait in your behavior conflicts with the above? 5a) What kind of (your name) do your colleagues, associates, or business partners expect? Describe. 5b) What secret or hidden trait in your behavior conflicts with the above? 6a) What kind of (your name) does society expect? Describe. 6b) What secret or hidden trait in your behavior conflicts with the above? 36 Please be sure to answer all of the questions. If you have any doubt about how to do it, see the box below for an example in which I pretend that I am a salesperson named Joe Brown: Answering these questions will help clarify which things you have to change in order to get past the Turning Point. --- Well done. You have analyzed yourself according to the expectations that others have of you. Now gather all the answers you wrote for part b) of the questions. These are the behaviors that need to change. If you keep doing them, and not what is rightly expected of you, you'll never make it past this level. The people who can give you opportunities will spot these shortcomings from a distance, and will be sure to leave you. Your network of alliances will be decimated. Without addressing these things, no matter how hard you may otherwise try, you will be unable to stay a great human being. Actually, allow me to be harsh with you for your own good: If you do not change these things that you have highlighted within the next year, you will no longer be a great human being, you'll just be someone who is pretending to be. Know that, no matter how many techniques you learn, how many books you read, how hard you work, the very shortcomings you just indicated will continue to emerge complicate your life. Not only that, if you persist on your path to success without changing them, they will notoriously become your trademark. Now you have to make a difficult choice. You can throw away this book, just like you threw away all the advice your good friends gave you, and try to smother everything you've read or thought with an avalanche of excuses. In which case you already know what awaits you: becoming invisible again. Or, you can use YOUR COURAGE and, while still being a simple human like everyone else, find the strength to rediscover yourself and be your very best. Success is not possible as long as you continue to betray the fair expectations of those who believe in you. If you want things to change, first you have to change yourself. Otherwise everything else is useless.

What kind of Joe Brown do the customers of your company expect? Describe. They would expect a very competent Joe, someone who prepares and searches incessantly for new technologies to satisfy them. An ally that offers new ideas and products to improve their company. A person who cares about their success. Who, after making a sale, does not abandon the customer but on the contrary, ensures that they will successfully use what they purchased, promptly solving any and all problems. Not just a salesperson, but also a friend, a business partner, and someone who actually takes care of them. 2b) What secret or hidden trait in your behavior conflicts with the above? I actually don't know much about the products I sell. I only really know a couple of them well and always sell those. When I sell, rather than focusing on the success of the client, I'm concentrating more on my sales and am not always sure that what I sell them will really work for their situation. I can't say I consider myself a "business partner" for the client, instead I'm mostly dedicated to selling my high commission products as much as possible. Also, I don't spend much time preparing myself technically. I am not aware of the latest market trends and as such am not always able to provide good service.

CHAPTER SEVEN

Become a leader!

Before reading on, have you completed the exercise in rule five? If you haven't, please do it now. Otherwise you won't get all the benefits of rule six. What happens to a person when they stop making excuses for their weaknesses? They will start noticing all the shortcomings of the other people around them. If you have worked well on the fifth rule, you'll actually start to see that some of the nonoptimal behavior and weaknesses that you had previously justified are also present in people around you. If you don't do something to help these people improve, if you simply put up with them, like it or not they will affect you, demotivate you, and rope you back into making the same mistakes that you just took care of in rule five. The world we live in is based on a firm rule: if you see someone doing something suboptimal and don't do anything to correct it, you'll end up doing bad things yourself. Whenever you accept something suboptimal in others, you yourself will change. I see this rule in action with business owners. For example, a business owner notices an employee is rude to customers. If she doesn't do something to handle it, or fails to influence it, she will simply end up resigning herself to it and, upon accepting it, begin to behave in a suboptimal way herself. It also happens among employees. An employee notes that the boss is always disorganized. If they don't do something to influence it, after a while they start to think that "it's not worth it" or "what's the point? Nothing ever changes anyway". Then they fall into the pattern of just doing the bare minimum, or only working because they "have to" without drawing any more pleasure from what they do. After a while they invariably try to compensate for the lack of satisfaction at work with other activities. Having failed to influence someone important in their lives, they themselves start to go downhill. When we see the shortcomings in another person we have two paths: either we influence them positively, or they will influence us, causing us to lose motivation and therefore dragging us down with them. By applying the fifth rule, really taking a close look at ourselves, we have already made a great leap forward. Now we have to follow this up by creating change in the people who surround us as well, otherwise the change that we have created for ourselves will not last long. This is the reason why the sixth rule of success is BECOME A LEADER! In fact, this is the only solution that remains in order to pass the Turning Point. If, after managing our own weaknesses or shortcomings, we do not learn to positively influence the people that are around us, they will demotivate us and, like it or not, will drag us back down. Soon we will again start making the same mistakes we had worked so hard to overcome in rule five. Becoming a leader 39 Leaders are the origin of positive changes around them. A leader is someone who, before anyone else, realizes that something has to change and then, having first changed it in himself, begins to promote those same positive changes in the people around him. In the '60s Martin Luther King realized that the time had come to speak out about the inequality between black and white Americans, and therefore decided that he would never again allow himself to be discriminated against. From there he began promoting that same change in his friends, in his acquaintances and, in the long run, in the United States of America. The path to becoming a leader begins with someone who realizes that there is something in their own behavior that could be improved. After making the changes described in rule five, the leader then continues by influencing other people until they too start to question their own behavior. If the process fails, their transformation into a leader will be interrupted, and they will fall back into invisibility. If they succeed, their full potential is brought to light and they become ever stronger and more respected. Taking on the responsibility of changing your own suboptimal behavior makes it even easier for you to appreciate the situations of the people around you. While you yourself are turning into an eagle, your sight will be honing in on other people, and you might not like what you see. At this point you have to become a leader for them and strive to promote positive changes around you. The responsibility of a leader A leader is someone who takes full responsibility for the behavior of others. Most people in society, when they see something that isn't right, will simply criticize, complain, attack, and demotivate. Leaders, meanwhile, don't bother with any of this because they realize that IT'S UP TO THEM to fix it. It's up to them to actually solve a problem that other people just complain about. Consequently, true leaders rarely criticize their surroundings. They know that the problem exists only because THEY haven't yet done anything about it, so the primary responsibility rests with themselves and not with other people. A leader in a company won't criticize a colleague's shortcomings, but acknowledge that her peers are acting in that (incorrect) way because she hasn't yet shown them how behaving differently could be more beneficial. A leader is someone who considers himself the main cause of how people around him behave. If his colleagues make a mistake, he does not criticize or attack them. This doesn't mean he's ok with the situation, he just recognizes that any failure on the part of his peers inevitably comes down to him. Leaders consider themselves the cause of any defects, deficiencies or weaknesses of the people around them. This is not about taking the blame. Assigning blame is something people do when they have such a low opinion of themselves that they can no longer influence their surroundings. Leaders do not attribute blame, because they know that doing so is useless. When they see something suboptimal, leaders take responsibility, knowing that it's only suboptimal because they still haven't acted yet. This not only allows them to constantly develop and improve their skills, but it also means that their attitude towards other people is positive and motivating, a guiding force and certainly not an accusatory one. 39 Leaders are the origin of positive changes around them. A leader is someone who, before anyone else, realizes that something has to change and then, having first changed it in himself, begins to promote those same positive changes in the people around him. In the '60s Martin Luther King realized that the time had come to speak out about the inequality between black and white Americans, and therefore decided that he would never again allow himself to be discriminated against. From there he began promoting that same change in his friends, in his acquaintances and, in the long run, in the United States of America. The path to becoming a leader begins with someone who realizes that there is something in their own behavior that could be improved. After making the changes described in rule five, the leader then continues by influencing other people until they too start to question their own behavior. If the process fails, their transformation into a leader will be interrupted, and they will fall back into invisibility. If they succeed, their full potential is brought to light and they become ever stronger and more respected. Taking on the responsibility of changing your own suboptimal behavior makes it even easier for you to appreciate the situations of the people around you. While you yourself are turning into an eagle, your sight will be honing in on other people, and you might not like what you see. At this point you have to become a leader for them and strive to promote positive changes around you. The responsibility of a leader A leader is someone who takes full responsibility for the behavior of others. Most people in society, when they see something that isn't right, will simply criticize, complain, attack, and demotivate. Leaders, meanwhile, don't bother with any of this because they realize that IT'S UP TO THEM to fix it. It's up to them to actually solve a problem that other people just complain about. Consequently, true leaders rarely criticize their surroundings. They know that the problem exists only because THEY haven't yet done anything about it, so the primary responsibility rests with themselves and not with other people. A leader in a company won't criticize a colleague's shortcomings, but acknowledge that her peers are acting in that (incorrect) way because she hasn't yet shown them how behaving differently could be more beneficial. A leader is someone who considers himself the main cause of how people around him behave. If his colleagues make a mistake, he does not criticize or attack them. This doesn't mean he's ok with the situation, he just recognizes that any failure on the part of his peers inevitably comes down to him. Leaders consider themselves the cause of any defects, deficiencies or weaknesses of the people around them. This is not about taking the blame. Assigning blame is something people do when they have such a low opinion of themselves that they can no longer influence their surroundings. Leaders do not attribute blame, because they know that doing so is useless. When they see something suboptimal, leaders take responsibility, knowing that it's only suboptimal because they still haven't acted yet. This not only allows them to constantly develop and improve their skills, but it also means that their attitude towards other people is positive and motivating, a guiding force and certainly not an accusatory one. 40 We call this special approach "causativity": the ability to see oneself as the cause of, or the potential solution for, negative events. Respect Leadership is not something that comes from a diploma or degree. Leadership does not come from our position in the company. Leadership is something that others recognize in us. We are recognized when people look at us and see our very best characteristics, with almost no defects. This is why it is so crucial to question yourself and eliminate the weaknesses you have identified in rule five. Without that step you will lack the foundation to become a leader. People will see your shortcomings and, if you continue to justify them, will never respect you. And if they don't respect you, it will be difficult to get them to perform as you wish, no matter the authority that comes from your position. After you've built a solid foundation, the second ingredient is to consider yourself the cause. Believe that the shortcomings, flaws or failings of others depend on you. By acting in the fashion you will become stronger and stronger. Do you believe in yourself enough that you are able to consider yourself the cause of what happens around you, or do you have such a low opinion of yourself that you feel compelled to place blame? Causativity begets causativity When you are causative with others, when you behave as if the problem depends on you rather than on your peer, after a while the majority of your peers will pick up the same behavior. If I have an argument with a co-worker and I blame her, counting all of her mistakes, she will tend to reflect my own attitude, just like a mirror. In her own turn (even though she may not say it to my face) she will think that I am actually the one who was mistaken. If, instead, I approach the situation with the clear message that there is no need to place any blame, and that maybe I myself have some responsibility for what happened, I not only maintain my attractive personality (because I don't get angry), but above all, after setting this example two or three times, my colleague will also start thinking that maybe she could have done things differently too. My causativity is mirrored in her. A manager who does not adopt causativity will create a team of people who, reflecting the same attitude as their manager, feel they are mere "effects" of their environment. It is no coincidence then that salespeople who are managed by an accusatory, demotivating sales manager, in their turn tend to find scapegoats to "explain away" their mediocre performance by blaming the customers, the recession, the shortcomings of the manufacturing department, the new president, etc. The sales manager's non-causative attitude is reflected in the sales team. 41 Be the spark of change You are becoming a new person, and therefore you can now also very clearly see the shortcomings of the people around you. If you want to continue on this path you have to become a leader, and to do so you have to abandon the "blame game" and believe that the shortcomings or problems around you depend on you yourself. If, for instance, there are shortcomings among your employees, don't criticize, but accept that it depends on you, that you still haven't properly conveyed to your employee the advantages or disadvantages of their behavior. If the situation is with a family member, again don't try to blame, but tell the other person that you realize you've let them down a bit by not helping them to improve. If it's with a customer, don't go to them full of critical thoughts. Think about what YOU could have done differently to ensure that things went better. Remember that 95% of times where things don't go as we would like because of the negative behavior of other people, there is still some way we could have behaved differently to prevent the situation. This way of thinking and acting will not only make you much more effective, but will also unleash a true internal revolution that will make you feel much more better. A study conducted by Dr. Mc Caw at the University of Montana in 1999 proved that the resulting job satisfaction of when you feel solely and directly responsible for the results of your work improves by 34%, however things go, while it decreases when you believe someone or something else is more responsible for what happened. How many attempts should I make to influence other people? If you try to be causative, you'll find that the majority of people around you will begin to change and improve, further strengthening your network of alliances. However, keep in mind that in society there is a percentage (3-8%) of people who will not improve despite your causativity. They are "toxic people". They're harmful because, after failing to achieve any improvement with them, you will start to question whether your causative approach really works and it will then cause you to regress. Perhaps it is contact with one of these people that has stopped you from using causativity in the first place. How can you tell if someone is a toxic person? By noticing that you're not getting any improvements out of them despite REALLY trying to be causative with them three or four times. The term "toxic people" does not mean that they should be criminalized or ostracized. They might actually be decent people (although they certainly aren't with you), but if they are not willing to question themselves, to be more honest in their relationships with others, you will find that they are not the best traveling companions on your journey to success.

CHAPTER EIGHT

The companions you choose determine your destiny: avoid toxic people

"To become the best in your field, you need to associate with the best. You must know that the companions you choose will determine your future" Brian Tracy If you associate with the wrong people, you can try to be as causative as you want but you will still fail in life. What can be done about that 3-8% of people in society who simply do not want to change? What can be done about the people you've tried to influence by taking responsibility for situations, using a win-win mentality, becoming a better person, but who still don't change and continue to make your life difficult? Well, know that there are only two things that can happen: either you find a way to influence them... or they will eventually start to influence and affect you. There are no alternatives. If you are unable to recognize this kind of person, they will make your life miserable. Pay close attention now because what I'm about to say is of utmost importance. Toxic People There are some people in society that are harmful to others. Whenever you associate with them, things tend to get worse. If there is such a thing as bad luck, it's actually association with one of these people. Every time in my life when I associated with such people, things soon started going inexplicably bad. I started making stupid mistakes, and the more time that passed the less confidence I would have in myself. Toxic people are like those huge trees, that block sunlight from all of the plants around them, and any little plants that do manage to survive are still weak. Association with this type of person entails great difficulties and certainly a great deal of stress. Furthermore, Dr. Michael Roizen, in his book "Real Age", says that if you consistently lose motivation due to constant bickering and conflict with people around you, the stress of it will reduce your life expectancy by at least eight years. Therefore avoiding toxic people is not just something that might help you be successful, it can also give you a longer life. So let's investigate the characteristics of people who turn out to be "toxic" for someone who wants to achieve success, or even just wants to survive People who are always negative There are people who focus primarily on the negative side of those around them. Have you ever had to deal with someone who, no matter what you did, always found something to criticize? Or who was always ready to point out everything you did wrong, without being equally ready to recognize all that you did well? Know that if someone is REALLY your friend, even if they point out your weaknesses, they will also be very generous with compliments for all the things that you do well. When there's good and bad news, you can be sure that the toxic person will only remember to pass on the bad. (The manager who tells their sales team "the boss is really angry that our numbers are down in California", when what you actually said was "things look great in Oregon and Washington, we just need to keep an eye on California".) Unfortunately they are unable to recognize this behavior in themselves, and if you point it out they either become defensive ("I'm just trying to look out for you", "If I don't say it who will?", "I'm just being realistic") or they lash out in denial. You'll probably even see that you're not the only one struggling. Other people near them will also find that their lives have become "inexplicably" more complicated and difficult. Being involved with a person like this for any extended period of time is frustrating, because it drains you, discourages you, makes you uncertain regarding your true abilities. It is no coincidence that people close to this person are often failing or have significant problems in their lives. Though toxic people might complain about how miserable all their friends are, the actual fact is that their negativity itself is primarily responsible for the dismal performance of their companions. It's like a steady drip of water that slowly, but insistently, wears a hole into stone. You can't help it: If you stay with them, they'll just make you weaker and weaker. People with a poor sense of ethics There are people who are often involved in unethical activities. It doesn't have to be outright criminal activity, it can be as simple as cheating, stealing, or lying. Being unethical can mean neglecting your work, cheating on your spouse, going back on your word, lying, scamming or take advantage of others. It doesn't matter how many justifications they might have for their behavior, you'll discover for yourself that people with a poor sense of ethics simply turn out to be bad companions. If they cheat on their spouse or lie to friends, then you can be sure that sooner or later they will do the same to you. But that should be the least of your worries. In the long run, continued contact with people like them will cause you to experience a worsening of your own sense of ethics, and your life will thus simply become more tangled. People who simply do not change or improve 43 People who are always negative There are people who focus primarily on the negative side of those around them. Have you ever had to deal with someone who, no matter what you did, always found something to criticize? Or who was always ready to point out everything you did wrong, without being equally ready to recognize all that you did well? Know that if someone is REALLY your friend, even if they point out your weaknesses, they will also be very generous with compliments for all the things that you do well. When there's good and bad news, you can be sure that the toxic person will only remember to pass on the bad. (The manager who tells their sales team "the boss is really angry that our numbers are down in California", when what you actually said was "things look great in Oregon and Washington, we just need to keep an eye on California".) Unfortunately they are unable to recognize this behavior in themselves, and if you point it out they either become defensive ("I'm just trying to look out for you", "If I don't say it who will?", "I'm just being realistic") or they lash out in denial. You'll probably even see that you're not the only one struggling. Other people near them will also find that their lives have become "inexplicably" more complicated and difficult. Being involved with a person like this for any extended period of time is frustrating, because it drains you, discourages you, makes you uncertain regarding your true abilities. It is no coincidence that people close to this person are often failing or have significant problems in their lives. Though toxic people might complain about how miserable all their friends are, the actual fact is that their negativity itself is primarily responsible for the dismal performance of their companions. It's like a steady drip of water that slowly, but insistently, wears a hole into stone. You can't help it: If you stay with them, they'll just make you weaker and weaker. People with a poor sense of ethics There are people who are often involved in unethical activities. It doesn't have to be outright criminal activity, it can be as simple as cheating, stealing, or lying. Being unethical can mean neglecting your work, cheating on your spouse, going back on your word, lying, scamming or take advantage of others. It doesn't matter how many justifications they might have for their behavior, you'll discover for yourself that people with a poor sense of ethics simply turn out to be bad companions. If they cheat on their spouse or lie to friends, then you can be sure that sooner or later they will do the same to you. But that should be the least of your worries. In the long run, continued contact with people like them will cause you to experience a worsening of your own sense of ethics, and your life will thus simply become more tangled. People who simply do not change or improve 44 There are some people who never question themselves. When you try to correct them or you point something out to them, they either pretend to humor you (while continuing to behave the same as always) or turn it back onto you and claim that you are actually the one who's wrong or the one who doesn't understand. Watch out for these people, because the longer you associate with them, the more their obstinate refusal to acknowledge their faults will cause you to start questioning yourself. And after constant association with them you will inevitably end up wondering, "Maybe they're right, maybe I am the problem...". If you continue to accept injustice, you'll start to believe that maybe it isn't unjust after all People who do not believe in you To be successful you have to have close friends who believe in you. This doesn't mean they always insist that everything is always great and that you never do anything wrong, but they are those who truly believe in you and your abilities. However you cut it, people who do not believe in you are not good friends, because they will merely highlight all of your flaws and amplify them. The people you spend most of your time with need to believe in you! --- When you're dealing with people who have any of the four characteristics I just described, put up your firewall and be very careful! And if you really want to know the value of a friend, ask him to describe what he thinks of his associates. His answer will be a description of himself. Contagion Should you have people in your environment with any of the above mentioned features or, even worse, realize that you yourself have some of them, you must quickly act to fix the situation. Otherwise, just like a computer infected with a virus that starts sending infected e-mails to everyone in the address list, with time you too will start to adopt and use the same characteristics. By spending time with toxic people you'll pick up their negative vibrations: like it or not, you will gradually become like them. I remember reading a book about a father who always beat his son. Throughout the book it told of the unspeakable suffering that the child experienced, of all the abuses he had to endure, but the thing that struck me most was the ending: the son, grown up, behaved just like the father. This is your future unless you have the strength to recognize toxic people for what they are and stop the contagion. Contrary to what you might think, I am not saying you absolutely must banish these people from your life (you could do this, of course, and I must say that you would actually be much better off), and I am not saying that you should attack them for being what they are. These are primarily unhappy people, who may even be helped in some cases, and who 45 should certainly be pitied. They are to be pitied because their life is sad to the point of bleakness. Confronting them with causativity Do not attack them, do not start a war, do not list all their faults. In a positive way, ask them to change their behavior. Try it three or four times. Of course, while you do the above, you should also try to question your own part in things, maybe there's something you need to change about your own attitude. If you do not find a way to influence them, you already know how it will end: you will be the one who is influenced, and not only that: you will also slip right back into the same bad habits we discussed in rule five. Associating with toxic people will slowly lead you to believe that all of humanity is composed people like this. It's not true. There are also many good people out there, who are happy if you are successful, who want to help others, and seek to highlight the good and the positive, rather than taking advantage of others and being negative, dishonest, and gloomy. The companions you choose will determine your destiny. If you want to fly with the eagles, you have to stop hanging out with turkeys, and above all ... avoid the hunters.

THE MATERIALIZATION OF SUCCESS Create your future!

The power of your imagination

By properly applying the fifth, sixth and seventh rules of success, you will have made a significant leap. Not only are you now "visible" to people who can involve you in real opportunities, but you will also have eliminated from your life any factors that may slow you down, or worse, cause you to relapse. You have chosen to be ethical, to become a decent person. You have influenced the people around you using causativity, and have become a leader. You have learned to recognize who your true friends are, and which people you should let go of. Now you're ready, you can dream big. Before successfully completing the first seven rules of success, the goals you established were mostly escape fantasies. But now you're ready to set and reach big goals. All things are created twice Stephen Covey, the famous American personal improvement author, argued that all existing things are created twice, the first time in our heads, the second in reality. Your home today exists because once upon a time someone had the idea to build it and continued to believe in that idea despite the adverse circumstances they faced. If that person had not had the original idea, or if he had, but then changed his mind, instead giving in to the adverse circumstances (financial problems, debt, red tape, etc.), then your home would not exist today. Unless you establish a goal, no matter how hard you work you will always be missing that first crucial ingredient needed to change your life. Because your life can only change if you first fix clear objectives and then continue to believe in your ability to reach them, despite the adverse circumstances that arise. Without goals, your life will develop by default, constructed by random events, by the desires of other people around you or through coincidences. Living is like being in a boat in the middle of the ocean. If you don't set a route, the boat will be moved by the currents (i.e. the desires and goals of other people) and you'll get nowhere. Wishing and deciding Many people I know tell me they want to improve their lives. They want a new car, a better paying job, a bigger company, a nice house, money. They think about it, sometimes talk about it, "hoping" for something to happen that will enable them to materialize their wish. Nothing will change in this fashion. Wishing is not enough. We must DECIDE to achieve that goal. When we wish for something, we think about it or at most make half-hearted attempts. We are tied to the concept of "hope", we hope something will happen that puts us in a position to make 47 RULE 8 The power of your imagination By properly applying the fifth, sixth and seventh rules of success, you will have made a significant leap. Not only are you now "visible" to people who can involve you in real opportunities, but you will also have eliminated from your life any factors that may slow you down, or worse, cause you to relapse. You have chosen to be ethical, to become a decent person. You have influenced the people around you using causativity, and have become a leader. You have learned to recognize who your true friends are, and which people you should let go of. Now you're ready, you can dream big. Before successfully completing the first seven rules of success, the goals you established were mostly escape fantasies. But now you're ready to set and reach big goals. All things are created twice Stephen Covey, the famous American personal improvement author, argued that all existing things are created twice, the first time in our heads, the second in reality. Your home today exists because once upon a time someone had the idea to build it and continued to believe in that idea despite the adverse circumstances they faced. If that person had not had the original idea, or if he had, but then changed his mind, instead giving in to the adverse circumstances (financial problems, debt, red tape, etc.), then your home would not exist today. Unless you establish a goal, no matter how hard you work you will always be missing that first crucial ingredient needed to change your life. Because your life can only change if you first fix clear objectives and then continue to believe in your ability to reach them, despite the adverse circumstances that arise. Without goals, your life will develop by default, constructed by random events, by the desires of other people around you or through coincidences. Living is like being in a boat in the middle of the ocean. If you don't set a route, the boat will be moved by the currents (i.e. the desires and goals of other people) and you'll get nowhere. Wishing and deciding Many people I know tell me they want to improve their lives. They want a new car, a better paying job, a bigger company, a nice house, money. They think about it, sometimes talk about it, "hoping" for something to happen that will enable them to materialize their wish. Nothing will change in this fashion. Wishing is not enough. We must DECIDE to achieve that goal. When we wish for something, we think about it or at most make half-hearted attempts. We are tied to the concept of "hope", we hope something will happen that puts us in a position to make progress. But when we decide to do something, we really get into action and we create the ideal conditions to materialize our idea... even if these conditions didn't exist before George Bernard Shaw once said that "the people who get on in this world are the people who get up and look for the circumstances they want, and, if they can't find them, make them." When we decide to do something, we must first really focus our minds on it. If we decide to build a home, we begin to plan or sketch out what it should look like. When we decide to visit a holiday destination, we begin to look at maps, to gather information on how to get there, where to sleep, where we can go and how much it might cost. If we can't afford to go this year, then we fill our environment with things that will remind us of our goal, such as hanging a poster of the destination in the office, or writing it in big letters on our calendar. The first sign that we have truly decided to do something is when we begin to explore our idea in depth, we collect information, we ask real questions along the lines of "How do I get it?". And if we meet objections or difficulties, we think about how to overcome them rather than simply accept that it is impossible. Meanwhile, when we merely wish we could visit a destination, we may think that it would be nice to do one day, we may even get up the courage to look up a bit of information, but we are crippled by the fact that we have already decided that it can't be done. We have become "spectators" in the game of life. I know many people who have become "spectators." They no longer decide on goals, they merely sigh and "hope" that their wishes will be realized simply by a stroke of luck. They're no longer active members of the team, and every important thing that happens in their life is established elsewhere on the playing field, while they remain seated in the stands. Of course they cheer the rest of the team on, agonizing over what might or might not happen, hoping, crying, rejoicing, but they have charged others with the responsibility of determining change in the game of life. Stop being a "spectator" in your life. Instead of just thinking about where it would be nice to sail your boat, start pulling out maps NOW and start charting your course. Perhaps it won't be a perfect route, but you can only find out by actually getting started. You will certainly never find out just by moping around down on the deck. Go to the helm, trace out a route, and start acting. When asked what their biggest regrets have been in life, eight out of ten people will say that what they didn't do haunts them much more than any action they tried and failed at3. Which means: what you don't do today will be the largest cause of your unhappiness tomorrow, more so than any actions you try today that then go wrong. In the future your main regret will be all the things you could have accomplished but never actually tried to do. Take a second to really think about it. The time to act is not tomorrow. IT'S NOW. Obviously you should also keep the other rules of success in mind while you are establishing your goals. You can't just abandon your commitments and run away. You shouldn't desert the network of alliances that you've built. But at the same time don't allow these considerations to keep you from taking flight: you're an eagle now and you have to fly. Imagination is more important than your current condition The first time I was asked to write down my professional goals for the next five years I almost laughed, because it was a very rough period for me. I thought that the trainer asking me to do the exercise must be from another planet. "How can you ask me to set any ambitious goals?" I wanted to object. "Don't you know that I have no money? That my car is such a piece of junk that I don't even know if I'm going to make it home tonight? That life has just been hitting me harder and harder? How can I see past all of this negativity?". With time though, I realized that: imagination is more important than your current condition. No matter what your current circumstances are in life, even if you've been dealt some very bad cards, if you keep your ability to positively dream of a better future, well then, you can make it happen. We can say that man lives at the center of two specific environments: one is the mental environment (our dreams and our imagination), the other is the material environment (the reality that surrounds us). The mental universe COMMANDS what happens in the material universe. Our lives, our property, is nothing more than a mirror of the dominant thoughts that we have in our heads. I understand that it may seem hard to understand now, but each of us has the power to alter what happens in our lives, simply by exercising that (often atrophied) muscle known as imagination. With the power of your imagination, building your life using the principle of "all things are created twice, the first time in our mind" and asking yourself achievable (yet motivating) goals, you can do much to change the course of your existence. It does not matter if right now you are living through negative moments. If you don't believe me, consider the data from these studies: according to a study conducted in 2000 by Forsythe, to predict the productivity of a person, knowledge gained through experience in the workplace is six times more important than diplomas earned at school. Meaning that, if you haven't had the opportunity to go to school, you can make up for six years of studying in one year of work experience, if you decide that you really want to learn a certain vocation. According Werneck de Almeida, to determine a person's chances of success, others consider the person's optimism to be more important than their experience, and even more than their actual probability of achieving results. That is to say, even if you are inexperienced, if you can get excited, and your enthusiasm infects the people around you, then they will believe in you. According to Arrison, the actual, current, conduct of an employee (both inside and outside the company) is six times more accurate in predicting the performance that the employee will achieve, as compared to their past work history. Meaning that it's not your past that determines your future, it's what you decide to do today. Your imagination is more important than the present facts. Even if life has backed you into a corner, if you set new goals and begin to move towards them, persisting and believing in your ability to achieve them, then you can change the course of your existence. 49 these considerations to keep you from taking flight: you're an eagle now and you have to fly. Imagination is more important than your current condition The first time I was asked to write down my professional goals for the next five years I almost laughed, because it was a very rough period for me. I thought that the trainer asking me to do the exercise must be from another planet. "How can you ask me to set any ambitious goals?" I wanted to object. "Don't you know that I have no money? That my car is such a piece of junk that I don't even know if I'm going to make it home tonight? That life has just been hitting me harder and harder? How can I see past all of this negativity?". With time though, I realized that: imagination is more important than your current condition. No matter what your current circumstances are in life, even if you've been dealt some very bad cards, if you keep your ability to positively dream of a better future, well then, you can make it happen. We can say that man lives at the center of two specific environments: one is the mental environment (our dreams and our imagination), the other is the material environment (the reality that surrounds us). The mental universe COMMANDS what happens in the material universe. Our lives, our property, is nothing more than a mirror of the dominant thoughts that we have in our heads. I understand that it may seem hard to understand now, but each of us has the power to alter what happens in our lives, simply by exercising that (often atrophied) muscle known as imagination. With the power of your imagination, building your life using the principle of "all things are created twice, the first time in our mind" and asking yourself achievable (yet motivating) goals, you can do much to change the course of your existence. It does not matter if right now you are living through negative moments. If you don't believe me, consider the data from these studies: according to a study conducted in 2000 by Forsythe, to predict the productivity of a person, knowledge gained through experience in the workplace is six times more important than diplomas earned at school. Meaning that, if you haven't had the opportunity to go to school, you can make up for six years of studying in one year of work experience, if you decide that you really want to learn a certain vocation. According Werneck de Almeida, to determine a person's chances of success, others consider the person's optimism to be more important than their experience, and even more than their actual probability of achieving results. That is to say, even if you are inexperienced, if you can get excited, and your enthusiasm infects the people around you, then they will believe in you. According to Arrison, the actual, current, conduct of an employee (both inside and outside the company) is six times more accurate in predicting the performance that the employee will achieve, as compared to their past work history. Meaning that it's not your past that determines your future, it's what you decide to do today. Your imagination is more important than the present facts. Even if life has backed you into a corner, if you set new goals and begin to move towards them, persisting and believing in your ability to achieve them, then you can change the course of your existence. 50 Write down your goals Just as a captain of a ship in the middle of the ocean must chart the course in written form, you too need to WRITE your goals if you want to make the change from "spectator" to "participant" in your life. Writing down goals, in fact, is a first step that already accomplishes a lot of the work needed to materialize them. First, it allows you to really focus on them and get into the details. Second, a captain needs to refer to his map and notes to stay on course after a storm. You too can refer to the written goals you have decided to materialize in your life, and use them to get you back on track after a storm or even a hurricane (which I can assure you there will be plenty of) has pushed you off course. A study conducted in 1999 by Professor W. A. Howatt showed that people who write down their goals have 32% more chance of feeling that they are making progress in life, as compared to those who didn't write down goals. Furthermore, according to Howatt, people who set their own goals in concrete terms are 50% more likely to feel confident in their ability to realize them. That is to say, if you clearly write the goals you want to achieve in life, you will feel immediately much more motivated and much more able to reach them. Unfortunately, only 3% of people in society have written down their own goals and aspirations. A few years ago I learned of a study at Yale University with students who were attending their last year in Economics. They asked which of them had goals in life. Some answered in the affirmative. They then asked which of them had written down and saved their goals somewhere. Only 3% said that had written their goals somewhere. Well, twenty years later, this 3% earned more than all the remaining 97% put together. I am not saying that you can simply write down your goals and then you'll never have to work again. What I mean is that the fact of engaging in something, the fact of writing down goals and referring to them, even when the storms of life might push us far away from them, will probably free large amounts of energy and potential in you that would otherwise have remained dormant. Successful people have the ability to continue to imagine the achievement of their goals, even when the circumstances seem to indicate otherwise We have said before that by continuing to believe in your goals, not belittling or invalidating them because of small failures, sooner or later they will materialize. Whenever I am committed to a new project that motivates me, it strikes me that, soon after embarking on this new project, I will inevitably run into certain facts or situations that push me to "give up", to make me understand that "I will never be able to achieve that goal". Always. There is no area of my life that hasn't been subjected to this phenomenon. It happened when I decided to be a successful salesperson, it happened when I was building my business, and it even happened when I decided to start writing books. When I published my first book (The New Leaders, which later went on to sell over 100,000 copies), we made a test of the book distribution via the Internet to test how it would do on the market before even offering it to a publisher. We mailed all of our existing customers (at the time over 3000), asking those interested to order the book through our website. We had determined that eight weeks after shipping we would evaluate the results. 51 We were sure that, after reading the first chapter, customers would want to read the whole book. Well, after eight weeks, how many books did we sell? Two. A truly disappointing result. I was already planning to throw everything out the window when I recalled this rule of success. I decided I did not care if the communication hadn't achieved any results. The book would be successful. Four weeks later we reached 500 orders via internet. Three months after that we were up to several thousand and we didn't even have a publisher yet... Just a few weeks before I could have aborted the project, I could have said "perhaps I'm just not that good of a writer". If I had, you wouldn't be reading these words now. It's bizarre, but it seems that there is a great force in the universe which, once you've established a goal or a dream, starts to play with you and make you think that you can't reach it. It puts you in front of obstacles to convince you that what you're aiming for is not feasible. It does so in the form of small failures, the partners who abandon or betray you, bad news and so on, all of which aim to make you give up. During my path to success, in fact, I found myself stuck in events that threw me into depths of despair. It's a test. If you have the courage to continue to believe in your idea and keep following the other rules of success, sooner or later, that idea will materialize; if you give up, well, you already know how it will end. The material environment plays with you to change your mind. Don't let it. Always remember this rule of success, because the bigger the stakes, the greater the weapons that the material environment will use to dissuade you. Know, however, and for me this was a GREAT discovery, that by refusing to abandon your dream, and instead continuing to believe in it, well, YOU WILL REALIZE IT. Treasure the problems that you face for the experience they give you, but DO NOT DOUBT EVEN FOR A MOMENT YOUR ABILITY TO REALIZE THE GOAL YOU HAVE ESTABLISHED. According to W. Clement Stone, our mind contains a mechanism through which if you're able to imagine something, then you're also able to achieve it. I am not advocating that fierce stubbornness toward your goals will lead to success. You have to make careful evaluations, especially when you invest a lot of money (although the best businesses in history were created with almost zero external funding4) and must also comply with the other nine rules of success. But know that your ability to persist in believing in your initial dream, in your destination, it is an essential ingredient of success. You cannot achieve what you cannot imagine and, above all, once you've decided something you must have the COURAGE to persist in keeping the image that you have created for your future alive, despite any external circumstance that try to convince you otherwise . Remember, imagination is more important than your current circumstances. "When you decide to solve a problem, you may encounter resistance at the beginning, but if you stick to it and don't stop trying, you are sure to find the solution. The trouble with most people is that they quit before they start." Thomas Edison

However simple it may seem, this exercise can create a BIG change in your life and in your work. If you do this exercise and keep the sheet with you, in a year you'll be surprised. Six, sometimes seven, of the goals you have written on that piece of paper will have materialized. You yourself will experience an immediate increase in your enthusiasm and effectiveness. Sometimes the mere fact of having identified specific goals actually sets things in motion around you. Write your goals in concrete terms and trying to be as specific as possible. Do not write vague things like "earn a lot of money" or "get rich", but write exactly how much you've decided you want to earn. Don't write "be happier", write what you need to accomplish in order to be happy. Write things that motivate you, things that you like, but that are also attainable at the same time (that is, things that you will actually be capable of accomplishing). Keep your feet on the ground, but your head in the clouds. You can imagine goals for both you professional and personal life or family. But don't limit yourself to just writing them down. Decide to truly actualize what you write. Then take the sheet of paper with your goals and put it somewhere where you will see it every day. In a year you'll be surprised, but even now, just by doing this exercise, you will have done something great. You'll have joined that 3% of people who have clear goals and you will have created the first key ingredient that you need to change your destiny: to clearly visualize things in your mind. Do it. And do not limit yourself to just writing. Decide to actualize what you have written. The miracle of our imagination Each of us in our life performs miracles. We perform them when faced with seemingly insurmountable circumstances and yet continue to believe in our dreams, in our desires, and then look around one day to realize that our vision has been fulfilled. Even a street cleaner is living a miracle every day. He has the idea of a clean street, and continues to maintain that vision despite the piles of garbage that are particularly large that day and, persisting in his imagination, something materializes that tourists and passers-by will appreciate. A sculptor makes a miracle every day. He doesn't see the roughness of the rock he's working with, but keeps the image of the statue that he will obtain from it fixed in his mind and, bit by bit, produces something that will arouse emotion in everyone who sees it. We are beings equipped with a miraculous power: our imagination. Our imagination commands what will happen in the material world, but you should know that after establishing a goal or a dream, the universe around you will begin to play with you to change your mind. This is also a rule of the game. If you treasure the experience you accumulate, without belittling or mangling your dream, then you can achieve it. The moment you stop believing, you resign yourself to a life that will be determined by random events, the people you meet, what other people decide, the economic conditions that, alas, may be unfavorable. In other words, you will have left the playing field and will merely be watching from the bleachers. However, do not assume that resigning yourself to the bleachers will ease your suffering in some way. The game will go on and you will continue to rejoice or grieve the victories and failures, the only difference is that you have decided not to have a hand in determining the results. What would you do tomorrow if there was absolutely no possibility of failure? What you don't do today, in ten years, will be your greatest source of regret. Far more than any failure you should ever face. Remember that.

The time perspective

Before going any further, have you written your goals? If you still haven't, I ask that you please do so now. I want you to get the most out of this book and all its possible benefits, and if you try to read on without writing your goals you'll be missing an important ingredient. In this chapter we will learn another reason why it's so important to write them. Dr. Edward Banfield of Harvard University conducted a study of what he calls "upward financial mobility": A study of people who, starting from nothing, have managed to achieve enviable financial situations. After analyzing many of the factors that contribute to personal financial success, Banfield concluded that there was one factor that was more important than all the others. He called it the "time perspective." Banfield found that, in any society, people reach a large personal success and grow in direct proportion to the time horizon by which they see things, or the time frame which they take into account. Persons who reach higher social and economic levels make decisions and make sacrifices that may not repay them for months or even years, but in the medium to long term may provide amazing results. People at lower levels in society, on the other hand, are people who, whatever they do, are seeking instant gratification. Their time horizon is much more limited. They do not make actions that will give them great returns in the future, but merely carry out those activities that give them instant gratification. These are people who prefer to spend their Saturdays and evenings watching movies or going out with friends, rather than reading books to improve their professional skills. These are the salespeople who can't be bothered to "waste time" building a relationship with a customer who may one day give them a lot of business in the future, instead they prefer to just close the sale and move on. These are the business owners who, instead of staying a little later in the evening to teach their employees and thus obtaining valuable assistance in the future, limit themselves to "squeezing out" every last drop of work they can get out of their staff for now, and end up with a team of non-autonomous workers. The world is full people like these. The short time perspective kills companies who limit themselves to selling and delivering without innovation (see Nokia in recent times), kills the hopes of young workers who, instead of focusing on learning more about their profession from the best in the field, just try to get the most out of salary (I basically worked for free for four years in the USA in order to afford an innovative education). It kills the customer-supplier relationship because the supplier is short-sighted and, just for a quick profit, fails to maintain a positive rapport with the people they will have to continue doing business with in the future. It kills a promising manager's dreams who, instead of continuing their education by attending courses and reading good books, always give in to instant entertainment or television. I'm not saying you have to live as a hermit, with no free time except for reading books, working for nothing, and denying yourself the entertainment that you have earned. I'm just saying that you need to put your life into perspective, and that perspective is in the future. 55 The present depends on the choices and actions you've made in the past. You cannot change the present because it is too fleeting, and because you cannot change what you did in the past. You can only change the future, tomorrow, next month, next year, the next decade of your life. To change the future, you must act today. Perform the activities that will make a big difference to your life tomorrow or in five years. Only then will your life begin to change. Try to answer this question: what are the activities that if you did today, would make a big difference to your future? Make an actual list and ensure time every month to devote to these activities. The time perspective is part of each rule of success All of the above rules of success are based on the time perspective. In fact, we could say that a key part of each rule is the fact of postponing immediate gratification in favor of a much greater fulfillment in the future. For example, the first rule (Stop following false leads) tells us that to be successful you have to work and study hard in your profession today, rather than give in to the lure and gratification that you might get from chasing after the "next great opportunity". The third rule (improve your quality of exchange) tells us that if you work more than you are paid, if you don't give into the temptation of instant gratification, you will inevitably earn more than you do now. The fourth rule (Become a great human being) tells us that giving priority to the needs of a friend may not necessarily be rewarding in the short term, but in the long term it definitely will be. The fifth rule (first you must change yourself) tells us that violating agreements, while possibly rewarding in the short term, in the medium/long term will make you pay a much higher price in terms of stress, anxiety, worsening relationships, and loss of self-esteem. In short, all the rules of success have this concept of the future built in them, and are based on the fact that each of us has the power to change our own life, but only if we take action now to make a big difference in the months and years to come. To write this book, I had to postpone many forms of "instant gratification": I had to neglect my family a bit, I had to neglect some customers, I had to pass off some activities in the company that, if I had followed them more deeply, would definitely have gone better and would have earned me more money. I had to spend part of the summer writing, and then I had to take shorter holidays. So I paid a price, because to write it I had to give up many forms of instant gratification. That price, however, now that I'm at the end of the manuscript, is coming back to me one-hundred fold, and in the future will continue to pay me back. What are the activities that, if performed in the coming months, would make a big difference to your life and/or profession? How much time are you devoting to these activities? 55 The present depends on the choices and actions you've made in the past. You cannot change the present because it is too fleeting, and because you cannot change what you did in the past. You can only change the future, tomorrow, next month, next year, the next decade of your life. To change the future, you must act today. Perform the activities that will make a big difference to your life tomorrow or in five years. Only then will your life begin to change. Try to answer this question: what are the activities that if you did today, would make a big difference to your future? Make an actual list and ensure time every month to devote to these activities. The time perspective is part of each rule of success All of the above rules of success are based on the time perspective. In fact, we could say that a key part of each rule is the fact of postponing immediate gratification in favor of a much greater fulfillment in the future. For example, the first rule (Stop following false leads) tells us that to be successful you have to work and study hard in your profession today, rather than give in to the lure and gratification that you might get from chasing after the "next great opportunity". The third rule (improve your quality of exchange) tells us that if you work more than you are paid, if you don't give into the temptation of instant gratification, you will inevitably earn more than you do now. The fourth rule (Become a great human being) tells us that giving priority to the needs of a friend may not necessarily be rewarding in the short term, but in the long term it definitely will be. The fifth rule (first you must change yourself) tells us that violating agreements, while possibly rewarding in the short term, in the medium/long term will make you pay a much higher price in terms of stress, anxiety, worsening relationships, and loss of self-esteem. In short, all the rules of success have this concept of the future built in them, and are based on the fact that each of us has the power to change our own life, but only if we take action now to make a big difference in the months and years to come. To write this book, I had to postpone many forms of "instant gratification": I had to neglect my family a bit, I had to neglect some customers, I had to pass off some activities in the company that, if I had followed them more deeply, would definitely have gone better and would have earned me more money. I had to spend part of the summer writing, and then I had to take shorter holidays. So I paid a price, because to write it I had to give up many forms of instant gratification. That price, however, now that I'm at the end of the manuscript, is coming back to me one-hundred fold, and in the future will continue to pay me back. What are the activities that, if performed in the coming months, would make a big difference to your life and/or profession? How much time are you devoting to these activities? 56 Remember that these activities, more than anything else, will help change your life. The seed of opportunity If you follow the rules of success, you will be able to find a seed of opportunity in every negative event. This concept fascinates me. Most people still do not understand it. When I try to explain it, people give me a condescending look and say "Yeah yeah, I understand, be optimistic and learn to see the glass half full even in the face of failures." But this is not what I'm talking about. The seed of opportunity is something magical, almost divine. Because the seed of opportunity is always something you can only understand after the fact. It's never something you recognize in the heat of the moment when disaster strikes. You'll see it for what it is months or even years later. But you must know that to cultivate this seed you have to be a person who has decided to follow the rules of success. The concept of a seed of opportunity itself is: if you follow the rules of success, every disaster that strikes you will also bring with it a great opportunity that you will understand later. Many years ago, while living in the US, my life was not going well. No matter how hard I was trying to make it, to break through, to pursue success and happiness, things were not going the right way. Then in the summer of 1990, I was hit by a series of negative events: my then-girlfriend, with whom I had done important projects, cheated on me and left me for someone else. It was a terrible blow. A month later, one night while I was working hard, I saw a copy of an e-mail from my boss on the corporate intranet: unspeakable things about me. That I was negative, that I was working against everyone, that I was one of the biggest problems in the company. That was the knockout blow. I decided to leave the USA. You can imagine how I felt upon returning to Europe. I was confused, sad, and vehemently disagreed with how I was treated and what had happened. Ten years later, I have come to bless that moment. Because if I had never gone back to Europe I would never have met the many great people who have worked with me to achieve success, I would not have founded my own company, I would never have gotten the job I'm doing now. With time, the resentment has passed, indeed I have come to think that it was actually a luck thing that my then girlfriend cheated on me. Lucky that my boss sent me that e-mail. They were not bad luck, on the contrary they have brought me the best luck. I simply couldn't appreciate it at the time. In fact they got the ball rolling, determining the change in my life that would lead me to success. Only all these years later have I finally been able to recognize the seed of opportunity. A few years later I suffered another hard blow. I, a manager determined to work seventy hours a week, running a company that was growing strong throughout all of Europe, woke one night with paralyzed legs. I had a disc hernia that had deteriorated to the point that it completely immobilized me. I was immediately hospitalized, and then had to undergo surgery. The night that I was hospitalized, I thought about my life. I felt a great loneliness. I thought about my future: what would become of me? What would become of my company? Would it have the strength to continue without my help? After the surgery, the doctors were categorical:

a month in bed, three months of rest and rehabilitation, during which I was not allowed to drive. A frightening prospect. 57 What did I do in those three months trapped at home? I wrote a book, The New Leaders, which today has already sold more than one hundred thousand copies, which allowed me to make many new customers, and even resulted in requests to write others. When I presented my partner with the manuscript, he told me: "You should get a herniated disc every year." That which had originally presented itself as a disaster, actually brought with it a great opportunity, the opportunity to write a book that would later achieve great success. The seed of opportunity is a concept that has something of the divine about it. Any disaster that strikes you carries with it the seed of a great opportunity. You do not understand this at the time of the disaster, but if you act according to the rules of success, you put yourself in a position to discover it and use its benefits. Maybe today your life isn't going the way you want it to. Perhaps you were recently dealt a blow that sent you reeling. Know, however, that though at first glance things are apparently terrible, it also includes a seed, a great opportunity that life has given you. Whatever happens, HAVE THE COURAGE TO CONTINUE TO LIVE ACCORDING TO THE RULES OF SUCCESS.

CHAPTER TEN

The success of an individual is measured by the success of those around them

"In life you can have what you want if you just help enough other people get what they want" Zig Ziglar We come then to the final rule, which is also the most important: your success is determined by the success of the people that are around you. This is the hallmark of every leader. This is the hallmark of every great person who has ever lived on this planet. There is a sort of MacLeod effect (see the famous television series Highlander) which occurs, not by cutting off someone's head like in the show, but every time you help someone win. Every time you help someone develop their own skills and become a winner, their skills become part of you. The more people you help, the stronger you become. Don't believe me? Look at Mother Teresa, one of the greatest examples of twentieth century leadership: she had nothing, but in fact possessed everything, managed and controlled enormous wealth, drove an army of thousands of employees without ever hiring anyone. All of this just because she helped them. Following this rule, starting from nothing, nothing but a mass of poor and dying, she created perhaps the largest congregation that the Catholic Church has ever been able to create over the past centuries, an extraordinary army. Every time you help someone, you become stronger This sentence is definitely true because the person you have helped will now become part of your network of alliances, and as such will "conspire" with you to help you succeed. But if we only see it in this way we are still limiting ourselves. There is also a psychological effect. Think about the last time you really helped someone. How did you feel afterwards?

Energized, happy, inspired. In fact, when you help someone to succeed in an area, through a kind of transfer you in turn become more proficient in the same area. This isn't hocus pocus, it's just a fact. If you help a plumber's apprentice to learn the secrets of the trade, you too, by necessity, will become a better plumber. Whenever I teach people management, for example, if my students effectively grasp the material something extraordinary happens in me: I at once feel that I have also improved in that subject. It is fascinating: by giving to someone else, you actually give something to yourself. The road to success The world is based on a balance of give and take. You can never pull out of this world more than what you put in to it. If you want something, you in your turn have to give something. If you want to succeed, you have to give success. If you want to earn money, you have to help others earn money, if you want love, you have to give love. 59 RULE 10 The success of an individual is measured by the success of those around them "In life you can have what you want if you just help enough other people get what they want" Zig Ziglar We come then to the final rule, which is also the most important: your success is determined by the success of the people that are around you. This is the hallmark of every leader. This is the hallmark of every great person who has ever lived on this planet. There is a sort of MacLeod effect (see the famous television series Highlander) which occurs, not by cutting off someone's head like in the show, but every time you help someone win. Every time you help someone develop their own skills and become a winner, their skills become part of you. The more people you help, the stronger you become. Don't believe me? Look at Mother Teresa, one of the greatest examples of twentieth century leadership: she had nothing, but in fact possessed everything, managed and controlled enormous wealth, drove an army of thousands of employees without ever hiring anyone. All of this just because she helped them. Following this rule, starting from nothing, nothing but a mass of poor and dying, she created perhaps the largest congregation that the Catholic Church has ever been able to create over the past centuries, an extraordinary army. Every time you help someone, you become stronger This sentence is definitely true because the person you have helped will now become part of your network of alliances, and as such will "conspire" with you to help you succeed. But if we only see it in this way we are still limiting ourselves. There is also a psychological effect. Think about the last time you really helped someone. How did you feel afterwards? Energized, happy, inspired. In fact, when you help someone to succeed in an area, through a kind of transfer you in turn become more proficient in the same area. This isn't hocus pocus, it's just a fact. If you help a plumber's apprentice to learn the secrets of the trade, you too, by necessity, will become a better plumber. Whenever I teach people management, for example, if my students effectively grasp the material something extraordinary happens in me: I at once feel that I have also improved in that subject. It is fascinating: by giving to someone else, you actually give something to yourself. The road to success The world is based on a balance of give and take. You can never pull out of this world more than what you put in to it. If you want something, you in your turn have to give something. If you want to succeed, you have to give success. If you want to earn money, you have to help others earn money, if you want love, you have to give love. 60 It may seem crazy, but if you can help someone else to achieve success, then you too will gain success. Have money problems? Work hard to ensure that your employees and customers earn money, and you'll see that, almost magically, you too will start earning much more money. This is the reason that rule three (exceed expectations) is so important. Whenever you impress someone with excellent service, your personality goes through a small but significant transformation: you become stronger. In the first chapter I said that success is not about escaping from an unsatisfying life, but about transforming your life into something great. Through the simple rules of this book we have seen what small, but significant, transformations each of us needs to apply. Transformations not of your work or of the people around you, but in your own personality. If you succeed in this metamorphosis, you'll see that, magically, your activities and the people around you will also be transformed. Success is actually a transformation of your personality. One small change after another, and one step at a time you will become a new person... and, like magic, you'll find yourself with a whole new life. The successful person Since we have spent the last ten chapters talking about how to achieve success, let's also discuss what this successful person looks like and how to recognize them. From their wealth? No. Saddam Hussein possessed palaces from Arabian Nights, nevertheless we wouldn't define him as a successful person. From their connections? No. We see many people in show business rubbing shoulders with many famous people, but when we look at their lives we can't call them successful. By their fame? Again no. Balotelli was a very famous and talented football player, but look where he is now. From power? No. Many business owners were very powerful figures, but ended their lives in torment. None of these features are distinctive signs of success. A successful person is recognized by the success of those around them. This is the true yardstick. You can always evaluate someone by looking at the people around them. Are those people successful? Are they happy? Are they financially prosperous? Have their lives improved since they entered this person's sphere of influence, or have they been getting worse? This is the hallmark of the true leader, the person who not only achieves material success, but also, and above all, spiritual success. If you see someone who is surrounded by people who are sad, unhappy or with many problems, you should realize that no matter how many enviable assets this person may have accumulated, they're on the wrong path. This is because they have built their success on a foundation of sand, and at the first bump in the road or change in economy their house of cards will collapse as quickly as it was built. Every day I see business owners or managers who have built companies made up of people who are afraid or weak. Every day I see individuals who, despite having obtained personal financial success, are surrounded by people who are doing poorly. And the closer I look, even as an avid supporter of the free market and capitalist initiative, the more I realize that their version of "success" just wouldn't do it for me. It would not work because it is independent from what is perhaps the most important rule: true success is based on the success of those around you. 61 This does not mean that we have to fall back on a socialist mentality or create big state cooperatives. They've tried that, and it didn't work. Instead, we must be aware of the great mission that has been entrusted to each of us. Each of us has a part to give to this world. Each of us must contribute a piece of the puzzle in building a new world, maybe even a utopia, but definitely better than we have now. And to do that, we must for a moment forget about OUR needs and look a little more to those of our neighbor. This book and my own life are small and humble examples that doing so is not only rewarding, but also allows you yourself to become a winner in your own time. Writing this book has cost me months of hard work that I've taken away from my profession, my family and my free time. But no matter how many difficulties I faced while writing it, I persisted because I felt it was my duty to give my piece. Life had given me so much and I had to reciprocate in some way. My piece of the puzzle is now out on the table. The world is now waiting for yours.